Live Rich on a Small Income

By D. S. Taylor

Illustrated by BNB Design

da house publishing April, 2013

ISBN: 1484160479
ISBN-13: 978-1484160473

Dedication

This is dedicated to Abby, who gave up her fine china and elegant living room to live in a larger America. Traveling more than eight thousand miles each year visiting friends, family, and finding "new," old places.

TABLE OF CONTENT

Acknowledgements

The great plan layouts in this book are the work of BNB Design (owners Andrea and Jeff Ballard.) They have interpreted my somewhat crude designs, into buildable home plans. Without their help this work may never have seen the light of day. Thanks guys.

Making the 20,000 plus words found in these pages digestible, with comas in the right place, and each sentence making some sort of sense to the reader has been the fine work of my editor Margaret Phares.

New Beginning

In the fall of 2012, the news media announced that 10,000 people are retiring each day.

There are many reasons people need or want to change their lifestyle. In today's economy many people simply want to downsize. Some reasons include: reduced income, retirement, just the desire to redirect their money toward new and different paths. That is to say they want to get more out of life. This then becomes a "New Beginning." The hope is that they will be able "To Live Rich on a Small Income."

When the kids are gone, work has become less satisfying, and your upward spiraling income seems to have slowed or stopped, what next? You need to plan for a new and different life. It takes a good deal of research and planning to maximize your life style, when your income slows from an avalanche to a mere trickle. By picking up this book you have actually started that research. Our goal here is to look at some ways to better spend your money, so that you can get the most out of life. The ideas presented in this book can help anyone, at any age, wanting to embark on a better life. Take charge; learn how to save money on the less important things in life, so you can spend money on that which brings more joy to your life.

The largest decision you will have to make at this stage of life is what to do about lodging going forward. If you have not downsized, this is a good time to start the process. Keep in mind that if you sell in a down market and buy in that down market, the transactions may offset each other. You benefit from downsizing and may acquire a smaller home in an area more desirable yet less pretentious area. A great house doesn't have to be a big house.

Downsizing can be quite different for different folks. If you have lived in 5,000 square feet for the past few years then a new home of only 1600 square feet will seem a drastic downsize.

When we contemplated retirement, we realized we could not "have it all." Choices would have to be made. Our family is spread out from Pennsylvania, West to Nevada and South to Florida and Texas. At that time we owned a very nice middle class home of 2,000 square feet. We sold that home and a lot of stuff we no longer required. After researching the RV market we decided on a mid-sized, top of the, line 5th wheel and Dodge one ton truck. Moving into 332 square feet and storage shed from 2,000 square feet was not without its problems. We also chose to retain our live aboard sailboat. It is not these possessions that make us rich but the life style we are afforded by keeping our dwelling small. We do not miss mowing the lawn, paying real-estate taxes or having a mortgage.

Where to start? Your home is probably the biggest investment of your entire life. First step: pick a much smaller house like one of our designs. Get estimates on land costs and building costs in a location of your choice. Next, see what the market will bring you for your current digs. Set your price realistically. Avoid the idea of getting top dollar in a down market. You may have to tread water for a bit, this need not be wasted time. Don't insist on having it now, two mortgages could kill your dream! Research the current market where you are selling and where you want to buy. Maybe research alternative sites.

Early on, you can begin divesting yourself of things you no longer use. Let's think about electrical things. Say you have recently purchased a new TV. The old one still works but has a smaller screen. SELL IT NOW before technology passes it by. This is especially true for cell phones, I phones, droids, and all of the personal communication / computing devices. Another good place to find money and reduce your storage is collections. If you have been a stamp collector or coin collector now may be a good time to sell out and apply the return to your retirement or travel fund. You may want to actually add to a collection before selling out. Get those stamps missing from a set, even if you have to pay a premium to acquire them. This could make the whole set worth more. On the other hand, sitting and staring at stamps, enjoying stamps for uniqueness and beauty may be your kind of great retirement.

Since your plan is to down size, this is the perfect time to CLEAN HOUSE! All that stuff you have been hoarding has to be sorted into "Gotta – Go" and "Gotta – Keep" This can be really hard. Just keep in mind your life will be much better if you do a really good job at this stage. An empty closet looks much bigger than a full one. Try selling on e-bay, have a yard sale, make a Good Will Donation! At one point Good Will politely ask us to stop!

 One good way to make this phase move forward is to rent several small storage (half) garages. Let's say three. Then label one Kitchen Stuff, the 2nd Furniture Stuff, and the third Hobby Stuff. If each costs $50 you can save $50 a month by eliminating just one. We did this and in about three months there was no storage cost! Put a sign on your bathroom mirror STORAGE COST $150 a month!

 Having a master plan is a good idea, but having intermediate goals will make achieving the dream possible. If you only have the dream without a plan, it is like looking into some other person's life, with little chance of actually living it! Set goals!! One really good thing about having intermediate goals is: you see progress. The thing about progress is, it inspires Progress.

How do you decide what must go and what must stay? Two good measuring sticks are time and value. Have you had it more than a year without using it, or you haven't seen it for several years, then maybe it should go. Does it have little value toward making your life better? Then it should go.

Do you really need the expense of two or more cars? Having two cars is a real convenience, but not having to garage the second one, pay insurance and maintenance could save you literally thousands each year. Selling one and using the money to allow a trade up of the second could net you one fine vehicle. On those occasions you really need a second car, rent one. Here is another place to be creative. Consider making a deal with a local car dealer or rental agent to rent a wreck or other model that isn't moving for them.

Selling your home can take some time. Ours took two years before we finally went to closing. Our plan included moving to a 5th wheel RV. We purchased that RV shortly after placing the house on the market. This proved to be a good move. It allowed us to live away from our house and keep the house inspection ready at all times. During this time we began seriously to divest ourselves of a mountain of stuff we would not require in our new life.

If your plan includes moving to fixed property and you need the cash from the sale of your house you will need a different plan. If at all possible, purchase the land and secure it for future construction. Do all the preparation possible to facilitate a short construction time. This will include at least having construction plans, selecting a builder and identifying the furniture and appliances you want. In short, know everything to be included, where to obtain it, color, model choices, and prices. Do this in writing. Planning at this level will reduce the time living in temporary accommodations.

When we downsized, our new home had primarily built in furniture. We sold some antiques to an antique dealer and had an auction of the rest of our unneeded household goods. If you choose to go this route, be prepared to accept the results. You will not get the price you think an item is worth in some cases. In other cases you will get more than expected. The good thing about this plan was that we were able to downsize rapidly, rather than over several months. We factored in thirty days between closing and possession by the new owners. Some buyers may not be so accommodating. Always ask.

Another aid to downsizing is to select a plan from this book that approximates your needs. Use it as a measuring device when deciding what you want to retain. If something would not fit in the space available then it should go. Keep in mind everything that must share the same space physical space. Remember you need some space for people.

When searching for a new boat we were taken with some that had a lot of beautiful, built in furniture. Upon reflection we realized there was little room left for people!

Just For the Young Adult

You aren't ready to retire, but still want to maximize life on a smaller income. While this book seems directed at those ready to retire, especially the baby-boomers, the concepts found here will help you achieve more in life than following the norm. There are a lot of seniors who wish someone had suggested Living Rich on a Small Income years earlier.

The baby-boomers, for the most part, followed a pattern from a rental apartment to owning a home that seemed to grow ever larger as their income grew. All the time paying mortgage interest while convincing themselves the tax deduction made it OKAY. All seemed well until the great real estate bust of 2008 and the years that followed.

There is a very old saying: Those who fail to learn from history are doomed to repeat it. Don't let this happen to you. In former times folks were expected to live up to their station in life. They had to exhibit outwardly not only the position they held, but the position they hoped to move next. Many a social climber has been caught on the way up by a road block and forced into bankruptcy. Things just happen.

When you get promoted it should be because of your performance, talent, or brains, not because you live in the right neighborhood. Yes that sounds naïve. Being promoted for superficial reasons will force you to constantly be on guard to do the right thing, live in the right neighborhood, wear the right clothes, and follow a lifestyle dictated by the boss. This can be a great formula for a heart attack! Don't wait for retirement to be your own person.

For many of us life tends to swallow us with routine. We decide to go to college or train for some job. Then love happens, we marry, and live in an apartment. Then it's on to a series of ever larger houses. One day we look around and wonder what else?

Want to get more from life? Break the mold! Do something to shake-up your life at least once a year. Get outside your shell. Travel to new or unusual places. Go sky diving, do a donkey ride down the Grand Canyon, climb a mountain, just experience life. You will be better able to do these things if you are not burdened with one of those back breaking mortgages. When contemplating any large purchase; house, car, even a home entertainment center, don't get yourself into oppressive debt. The two worst investments are interest and rent, once paid they are gone forever.

I've always wanted a 1962 Corvette and a sailboat. For a whole lot less I did get the sailboat and travel in Europe. Who knows, that Corvette is still on the Bucket List.

Selecting the Next Home

Many people move to condo style living when downsizing. When making this decision, factor in the added costs. Condo fees alone may make this prohibitive. Having all outside maintenance provided by the association may seem ideal, but is the service received worth the price? Later in this book we will discuss the economics of Doing-It-Yourself.

Assuming you have elected to have a fixed property as your next residence, I have included several plans for various size houses, ranging from 1600 square feet to less than 400 square feet. Some have three bedrooms, some only one bedroom, and even an efficient apartment style with a great room that turns into a bedroom. There are several concepts you need to be aware of:

1. Small homes are harder to keep in order.

2. Small homes have less storage space available.

3. Small homes have less room for large egos.

4. Compromise takes on new meaning when living in close quarters

If you and your mate have never shared a small living space, try it before you buy it. Rent a very small cottage, apartment, or an RV. This will help you find out how you react to bumping into each other, sharing a single bathroom, and dividing up limited storage space. While this will have some cost it could save you from moving into too small a space.

I'm not trying to discourage you from going small. There is a right size of small, unique to everyone, in which only you and your mate will be happy. You will find plans in this book of many different sizes of "Small." If you can be truly comfortable in a very small space, then you could consider living on the road or one of the very small cottages presented in this book.

The House and Shelter Plans in this Book

Let's face it, any house, is at the root, merely a shelter for its occupants and their stuff. How big or how grand the shelter is up to the owner and his/her accountant. The plans in this book show a range of shelters that can be appointed to make them quite grand while remaining small and efficient. Those appointments may include such things as stone counter tops to elevators. Actually you can drop tens of thousands of dollars in a kitchen alone. On the other hand, the basic idea of this book is to have the look of luxury at an affordable price.

Kitchen counter tops will be a good place to start. Of course there is granite near the top of the cost spectrum. In today's market there are numerous products marketed as solid surface counter top material. Corian is the best known and was among the first on the market. These look great and have the cold feel of real stone. They require little care, but unlike granite, do not sit a hot pot on them or drop a cast iron skillet or other heavy object in the middle of one. They are made-up of resin and various fillers and will scar or even crack. Those examples that have integral edges and borders of a contrasting color are especially appealing. This material is so versatile, sink bowls can actually be molded in to the counter top. I personally prefer the sink be a drop-in stainless steel type. Those molded sinks do have a certain luxury look, but stainless in the kitchen tends to say it is sterile and is easy to replace should problems arise.

Black and stainless appliances are very popular these days. When it comes to refrigerators, stoves and dishwashers, don't buy more than you need. Really large refrigerators tend to harbor large amounts of left-over's and other undesirables. A mature couple can survive nicely having a twelve or fourteen cubic foot refrigerator. Cooktops having 2, 3, or 4 burners with either gas fire or electric burner units are available. For many, one of these together with a convection / microwave will serve well for all cooking needs. If there are only two in residence an apartment size dishwasher will do nicely.

Generally all "Home Stores" have kitchen showcase displays and will order cabinets to fit your kitchen. If you order a complete kitchen from the same supplier you should ask for and receive a good discount on the whole package.

Eat-in kitchens and kitchens open to great rooms are featured in this book. When kitchens are included with great rooms the goal should be to compliment not contrast the living area.

Like many American families we probably eat-out way too often. On occasion we do split meals, but not often enough. Splitting meals not only saves money but also helps control weight gain. Speaking of food, when we are lucky enough to attend a potluck dinner and take some of mom's special pickles or home canned meat sauce, people seem amazed that we are able to can food in our small kitchen. It's the creativity and skill of the cook not the size of the kitchen that makes for great food.

Living the Concept

As a discerning person you would not want to follow the advice of a writer that had not walked the walk. My wife and I have lived in about 332 square feet of a 5th wheel trailer, with some time spent aboard our 30 foot sailboat, for the past eight years. We travel about 8,000 miles each year. We visit friends and family and make extensive side trips. Our income is indeed small, but we have learned how to stretch it by following many of the suggestions found in this book. We feel we have a very rich and full life. Happiness, like beauty, is in the eye of the beholder.

There is no doubt in my mind that we would (and may yet) find happiness in any of the homes represented in this book, provided it was in a great location. We value sunshine and prefer to visit snow rather than have snow visit us. By utilizing National Parks, desert plots, and monthly RV park rates, we have been able to keep our campground costs low. The biggest problem we have is planning to visit the Northwest, including Washington, Oregon, etc. and New England. The problem is that when the weather is friendly enough for travel to those regions it's sailing season! One of these years we will just have to forfeit some sailing and go.

Though it may be trite to say, "Life is What You Make of It," IT IS!"

No matter what new life-style you choose, remember you can meet and solve all those little problems that arise, because you are in-charge. The two most important tools you have are: Research and Planning.

Our House

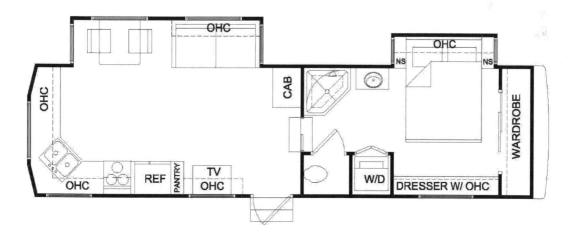

The Abby

This is undeniably a good looking basic home. It has all the essentials arranged in a very efficient pattern. That dormer, while the only purpose is to emit light into the garage, adds a special look to the home. The full width front porch, with square columns, makes for an elegant entrance. Full length windows in the living room and dining room provide bright and open entertaining areas. The addition of half height inside shutters will provide a margin of privacy yet allow opening up when desired.

Having a guest closet next to the front door is a real convenience. Want a larger guest closet? Turn it 90 degrees and expand it a couple of feet. You will still have a nice dining space, now with greater separation from the living room.

Moving on to the kitchen, we find an efficient U shape pattern. There is enough floor space to allow two people to prepare a meal together, without running each other down. You can cram in a lot of dishes, groceries, and stuff into all that cabinet space. The window to the dining room helps open up both spaces and aids in meal time communications.

When it's laundry time, you will find the location just off the kitchen to be very convenient. You can throw a load in the washer while preparing a meal and have it done by meals end. The bad thing about the convenience of the modern laundry is that you may become addicted to living out of your dryer!

The master bath is of reasonable size and would be enhanced by the addition of a sky lite / exhaust fan. That half bath is a must even in an economy two bedroom home. The location across from the guest room is a real convenience.

The master bedroom has generous square footage. Those well-placed windows allow for efficient furniture placement and plenty of light. The hanging closet at 7' 6" is of good size. Think of rooms like this as an artist's canvas waiting for the addition of color and form. Until you add these it is just a big rectangular box without much warmth or character.

The guest room has a head start on character with that bay wall and large window. It screams for duel use as a den / guest room. One possibility would be to apply a library look. Install a "Murphy Bed" to the wall adjoining the garage. Surround it with book cases reaching the ceiling. A couple of nice leather chairs placed at comfortable angles in the "bay window" area will add to the look. If you like, add two side windows to that bay and a small table between the chairs. The two car garage is not a must but just seems right in this design. Most homes this size have rather "Blah" rear elevations. That guest room bay window will add some charm to this otherwise characterless view of the house.

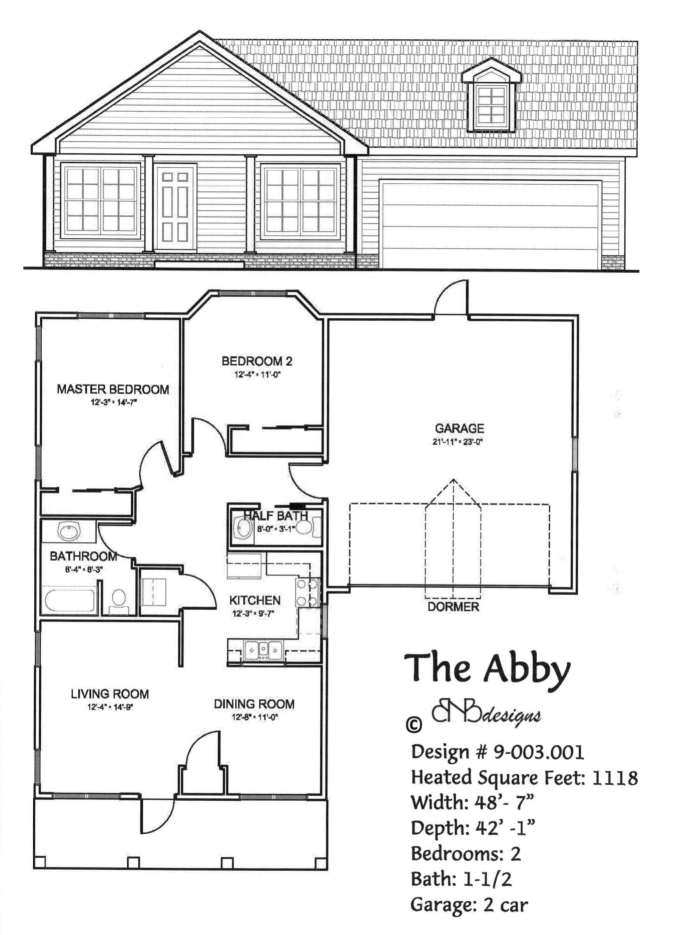

The Abby

© CNBdesigns

Design # 9-003.001
Heated Square Feet: 1118
Width: 48'- 7"
Depth: 42' -1"
Bedrooms: 2
Bath: 1-1/2
Garage: 2 car

MASTER BEDROOM
12'-3" × 14'-7"

BEDROOM 2
12'-4" × 11'-0"

GARAGE
21'-11" × 23'-0"

HALF BATH
8'-0" × 3'-1"

BATHROOM
8'-4" × 8'-3"

KITCHEN
12'-3" × 9'-7"

DORMER

LIVING ROOM
12'-4" × 14'-9"

DINING ROOM
12'-8" × 11'-0"

The Andrea

If you need three bedrooms, this one might just be for you. This house was designed to give the master bedroom maximum privacy. For a home of only 1500 square feet, it will feel much more spacious. Those two bathrooms have more of an open feeling than your typical closet style bathrooms. The central bath contains laundry equipment in a convenient location. The master bath features dual sinks and a separate toilet room. Add the large walk-in closet and you have an awesome master suite for a small home.

Bedrooms 2 and 3 are of good sizes and could have different roles. Either might serve as a library or den, while the other as a guest room. Should you expect frequent visits from your kids with their kids, the 3rd bedroom might be best outfitted with bunk beds. This would allow more floor space for play.

In today's economy, more and more families are having adult children move home for extended periods. Assigning the second bedroom for this purpose will give both the adult child and you a fair measure of privacy.

The kitchen design allows easy access to all appliances and has an enormous amount of counter space for meal preparation. There is a large amount of storage in both the upper and lower cabinets. Should you require even more storage, additional over counter cabinets can be installed above the island sink.

The great room has 325 square feet of living and entertaining space, with a large closet to boot. The obvious arrangement would have a dining table and chairs at the kitchen end. This would leave a large lounging area at the other end, which could be set up reflecting the owners taste.

The pillared front porch could be enlarged to accommodate patio-type furniture for those who enjoy "Front Porch Sit-n." The two-car garage is large enough to accommodate two of today's mid-sized cars or even an SUV and an economy car.

The elevation shown would fit in most parts of the country. Should you build in the Southwest this plan could be built with a typical, Spanish / Southwest, flat adobe roof, including exposed roof rafter poles.

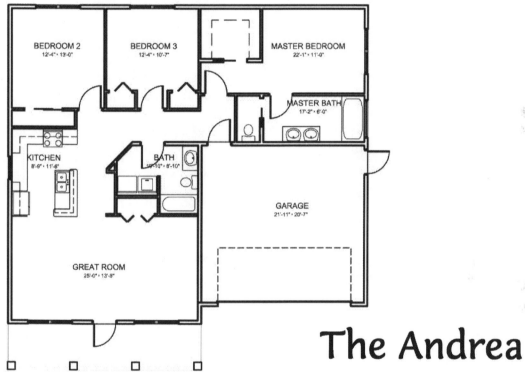

The Andrea

© *NBdesigns*

Design # 9-003.002
Heated Square Feet: 1514
Width: 48'- 7"
Depth: 42'- 1"
Bedrooms: 3
Bath: 2
Garage: 2 car

13

The Alexandra

This is one of my favorite designs and is therefore named for our granddaughter. Daughters are really great but granddaughters hold a special place. This design is special in many ways. All of the doorways are 36 inches wide. The master suite allows 36 inch passage throughout. While this may not satisfy some zoning definitions of wheel chair accessible, it is to say the least, wheel chair friendly.

Cramming a lot of living into a small area is indeed a challenge. For many, many years the kitchen was the busiest room in the home. In today's fast food, order out, and eat on the run world, not so much. Following the theme of this book, it seems only appropriate that this home and others in our collection have great rooms. In older, more spacious, designs the cook was banished to the kitchen, not to be heard from until a meal was on the table. Modern design trends have included windows and open counters to allow the cook to participate in the conversation or even to grasp a glimpse of the Super Bowl while preparing a meal. The great room also allows each space to feel larger while functioning in its specialized role. For example: at Thanksgiving the dining table can be extended to accommodate a large family, without cramming everyone into a walled space that is too small for comfort.

This particular design has no hallways. While hallways are necessary in larger designs to separate and define living spaces, they are otherwise simply wasted space. The inclusion of a separate master suite and a guest suite in this design provide full separation and privacy for each.

Of special interest is the master bath. It contains a full-sized whirlpool bath and full-size laundry equipment. Yet space has been allowed for parking a wheel chair alongside the toilet and bathtub.

Not quite enough space for you? This concept can be exploded up to 1,000 square feet, allowing even better handicap access. Don't need handicap access now? All of us may need it one day, and it adds to the resale value. Having handicap access would allow many seniors to remain in their own homes longer.

Let's move on to the all-important exterior look. Almost any floor plan can have several very different looks. This one looks good with the basic low country elevation. Note how the gabled ends tend to elongate the basic dwelling.

GARAGE
12'-6" × 18'-0"

BEDROOM
12'-6" × 10'-6"

BATH 2
7'-8" × 7'-5"

MASTER BEDROOM
13'-8" × 10'-5"

BATH 1
8'-11" × 11'-6"

GREAT ROOM
17'4" × 11'-6"

KITCHEN
10'-2" × 11'-6"

The Alexandra

© CNBdesigns

Design # 9-003.013
Heated Square Feet: 894
Width: 51'- 4"
Depth: 23'- 4"
Bedrooms: 2
Bath: 2
Garage: 1 Car

The Julianne

The Julianne is a great choice in a one-floor efficient plan. The front door is adjacent to the driveway eliminating the need for a separate front walk. That garage can be built as a patio /carport. As a garage, the addition of a back door and shelves at the far end would provide a lot of storage and access to the back yard. Alternatively this area could be equipped as a work shop.

The entry directly from the garage to the house makes for a short path for carrying groceries to the kitchen counter. This also eliminates dragging stuff through the living room area. That counter next to the living room area would serve well as a lunch counter.

The 15' X 17' living area opens up to the kitchen making both seem massive. If built with cathedral ceiling you would feel as though you were in a great hall. This great room is almost large enough to support an echo. The master bedroom suite and the guest suite are quite large by small house standards.

The master bedroom and bath are of sufficient size to be wheel chair friendly and include a large walk in (wheel in) closet. The guest suite is not large enough to be wheel chair friendly, but certainly is fully equipped and a good size for its intended purpose.

The kitchen at 15" X 13' is large by any standard and fully equipped to handle a large Christmas dinner. Add a large drop-leaf table along the garage wall in the great room, for just such occasions. You could serve eight for Christmas dinner.

While the drop-leaf table is parked alongside the garage wall, I'd suggest you hang a large flat screen TV above it. From this location the TV could be seen from all over the room, especially if mounted on one of those goose neck TV mounts.

All in all the Julianne is one really big small house.

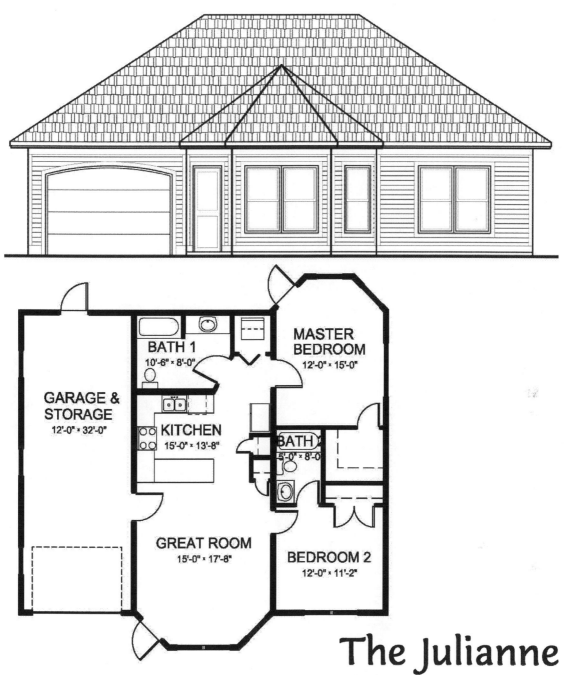

GARAGE & STORAGE
12'-0" × 32'-0"

BATH 1
10'-6" × 8'-0"

KITCHEN
15'-0" × 13'-8"

MASTER BEDROOM
12'-0" × 15'-0"

BATH 2
5'-0" × 8'-0"

GREAT ROOM
15'-0" × 17'-8"

BEDROOM 2
12'-0" × 11'-2"

The Julianne

© CNBdesigns

Design # 9-003.004.1
Heated Square Feet: 1032
Width: 41'- 3"
Depth: 40'- 8"
Bedrooms: 2
Bath: 2
Garage: 1 Car

Live Tall ~ Live Rich

The term mansion usually applies to a large two-story home. However, you can indeed feel rich living in a luxury small two-story home with a grand view. Why live tall and small? Because you want to enrich your life in other ways and not have your wealth consumed by a larger property. Living tall you get a smaller footprint which will actually save land and construction costs. Build a small-tall two bedroom like one of our designs with luxury appointments and you have a mini mansion. You could even add a barn outback, full of your favorite old cars, or maybe a hanger, a boat, or enough Harleys to have your own parade! The possibilities are endless.

Perhaps you are interested in a second small tall home as a cottage with auxiliary power in the Colorado Mountains or up near Santa Fe, New Mexico. Your second home can be anywhere. What a great view you would have from a second floor balcony in the mountains or near the beach!

Our small-tall designs can be very impressive and very comfortable with a few tricks learned from this book and other sources. Go against the tide. This kind of downsizing can by-pass cheap and avoid skimping on luxury details. When you build your small house, be sure to include appointments such as whirlpool tubs, granite counter tops, and the best cabinetry or whatever things you find luxurious. Living rich is more than the size of the home. It is content that truly signifies the wealth of the owners. Remember the view from a two-story can be a reason enough to choose "Living-Tall "

What it really comes down to is: Do you want to be wealthy or do you want to have a rich life? This contrast was best portrayed in the movie "It's A Wonderful Life." Mister Potter was very wealthy and lived in a mansion, but did not have a rich life. George Bailey on the other hand, had a very rich life while living in a large but modest home. A mini mansion can provide that rich feeling, without becoming a money pit.

It takes a great deal of planning and just plain forethought to maximize the return on your money. NOW is the best time to begin planning and doing research. Living TALL can certainly be a move in the right direction.

Go for the Gold

The Elevator

Why the heck would anyone want an elevator in a small house? Well, two-story homes allow a lot of bedroom privacy and also give you a view not available from a ranch. Look at it this way, a two-story needs less foundation and it has less roofing. This helps off-set the cost of an elevator.

As I get older it seems that someone adds pounds to the stuff I must lift and length and height to the stairs I must climb. Older people I know living in two-story homes look forward to the day they will no longer have to climb stairs. When planning your next home why not have all the advantages of a two story home and yet not have that daunting chore of having to climb stairs every time you want something from the bedroom? The elevator can provide an escape route from that garden club meeting or that poker game, and allow you some quiet time.

Our goal here is to design small luxurious homes.   Remember when Cadillac, Lincoln, and Buick were a block long and considered "luxury" cars? In the early 1960's Caddy's had fins that would make a jet fighter proud. At that time Mercedes-Benz was building much smaller luxury cars that were being enjoyed by many at the country club. These smaller autos had leather upholstery and fine furniture grade wood trim, exuding luxury in a more easily handled package.   That is what we aim to do, design small luxury homes that will have the very best components and yet be small and unique in design.

Many designs in this group will easily convert to allow wheel chair access ability. Why? Because we may all need it someday. It will add market value to the home.   This is the home to grow into your senior days without having to move to senior care. In the meantime, you can enjoy a luxurious bathroom and an easy up, easy down elevator. Won't your friends be jealous of that elevator?

There is an old saying, "He (or she) who dies with the most toys, wins." It does not say "he or she who had the biggest toys!" You can consider the elevator as one of those toys. While you are at it, remember that by having a smaller luxury home you can afford more toys. Let's say a boat or a motor home or an airplane or even a second small luxury home in a vacation land. How about a home in New England, or one in Florida and one in Arizona? These homes would look great in the Scottish Highlands or even make a nice Swiss chalet or Italian villa. Simply changing the front elevation to reflect the locale will make them fit in almost anywhere.

Now your only objection to that elevator may be, "What if the power fails?" This can be solved very easily with another toy. It is called an emergency (back-up) generator. Here again think small, don't let some fast talking sales person sell you 15,000 to 30,000 watts of power. I don't think you want to heat the pool by generator. Nor do you want to feed a generator that will light up Las Vegas simply to raise or lower that elevator, watch TV and pop popcorn in the microwave. Do a little research. Ask yourself, what are my needs during a commercial outage? You can't have it all at one time and you can't run all your appliances at one time either. But you can have what is most important to you.

That elevator will head the list of power needs during a black out. It will not require continuous power but must be considered when sizing an emergency generator. Second only to the elevator, in some areas, will be air conditioning. Here again, the small luxury home has it all over the larger home. Less air space, less air conditioning needed, therefore, a smaller air conditioner and generator.

Want to keep the cost low and still have emergency back up? A good answer here would be a UPS, which is an Uninterrupted Power Supply, not the United Parcel Service. These are basically a battery with an electronic control that keeps the batteries charged and automatically supplies power when commercial power fails. These are available from residential elevator suppliers.

The Beach House

An elevator can make accessibility to a raised beach dwelling available to those who have difficulty with stair climbing. The plan shown does not qualify as a two-story home, it is decidedly second story living. There are some real advantages to building such a raised structure. This home would afford great views in two directions from two porches. Properly constructed, it would meet local codes for storm surge protection. It would also have a lot of carport storage under the living area.

Luckily many elevators on the market today require minimal pits at the bottom and have most of their mechanical / electrical parts above the top floor. They would be above the storm surge line and relatively safe from water damage.

This design is shown as a one bedroom home, in keeping with the small house theme of this book. I'm quite sure BNB design would be happy to work up a two bedroom design based on the RAE LYNN concept shown on page 26.

This design could also be used in mountainous terrain by cutting into the side of a hill. It would require the installation of a retaining wall and proper drainage.

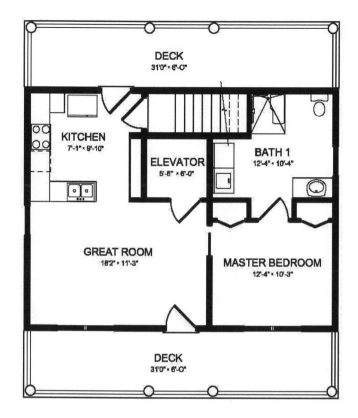

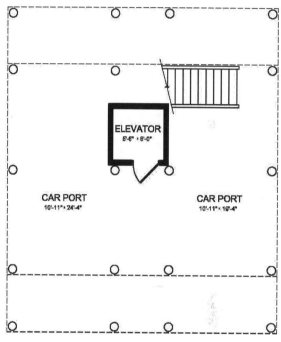

The Beach House

© *CNBdesigns*

Design # 9-003.012a
Heated Square Feet: 787
Width: 32'- 2"
Depth: 30'- 7"
Bedrooms: 1
Bath: 1
Carport: 2 Car

The Topper

Here is a compact two-story with a lot of luxury in the design. It has zone isolation, so welcome when you have overnight guests. All the rooms are of good size because we did not try to cram too much into the 1300 Square feet design goal. Two-story living is very inviting. Think of this home somewhere along the Intracoastal Waterway. What great scenery available because of the elevated view! Or, build this as a mountain retreat, with the ability to see more of the wonderful view around you.

When built facing south, the roof presents a great opportunity to go green by installing solar panels over the entire surface of the front roof. On this two-story, those solar panels will have better exposure to the sun than they would on a ranch house surrounded by trees. For maximum solar exposure it would be best to build with the roof ridge running as near east and west as possible.

Residential elevators allow second story living for those not normally able to climb stairs. As we get older, we are less and less inclined to want a home with stairs. Persons requiring the use of a wheel chair especially will want to avoid homes that cannot provide easy access to all areas. The two-story homes in this book are specifically designed to allow space for a residential elevator. Installing an elevator is not required. If omitted, the space is located to provide a useful storage closet. When and if the home exchanges owners, the new owner will have an easy install for an elevator. It should be noted, that with this design it would be a bit awkward having only the stairs in the garage to access the second floor. Reason enough to install an elevator.

There are several distinct advantages to a two-story home, including the construction savings gained by having both a smaller roof and smaller foundation. This will help offset the cost of that residential elevator. The Topper design allows for construction on a lot having less frontage, while still leaving space between houses. This could be a big cost savings. Heating and air conditioning a two story will provide ongoing savings. Quite simply, two-story homes are more efficient to both heat and air-condition.

The second story porch with access from the great room is a great place to enjoy dessert after a good meal. It also gives some weather protection to the front entry way. Not to mention the great look of those columns.

There are only two bedrooms, if you really need more, build one of our guest houses or build the big sister design THE RAE LYNN. It has three bedrooms and a two car garage.

The Topper

© CNBdesigns

Design # 9-003.012
Heated Square Feet: 1324
Width: 32'- 2"
Depth: 30'- 7"
Bedrooms: 2
Bath: 2
Garage: 1 Car

The Rae Lynn

The Rae Lynn is an expanded Topper with all the advantages of a two-story with three bedrooms and a two car garage. Because of the spacing required by the two car garage the columns had to be eliminated. To help reduce construction cost the balcony was also eliminated. It could be included as cantilevered balcony with a door in place of the central window as it is in the Topper plan.

The Rae Lynn

©

Design # 9-003.011
Heated Square Feet: 1585
Width: 39'- 10"
Depth: 25'- 10"
Bedrooms: 3
Bath: 2
Garage: 2 car

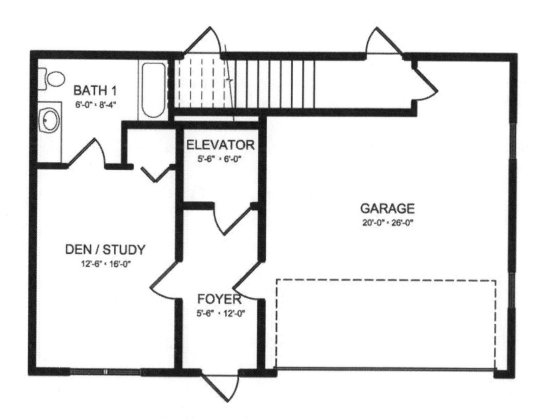

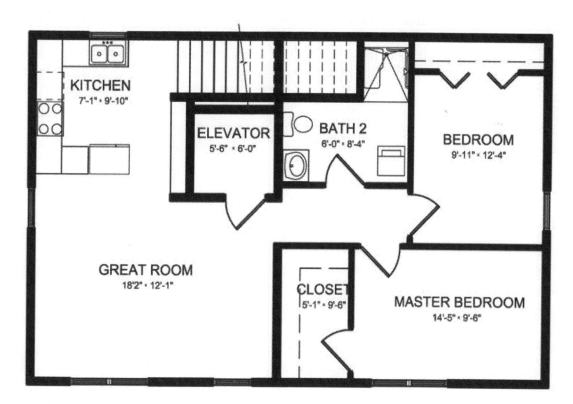

27

The Theodore

This design is definitely in the realm of classic Southern Plantation architecture. To be more specific it is very "Mount Vernon" in its exterior design. Two-story homes seem to rise and fall in popularity, but are always present in most communities. Having a two-story home implies one of two things: either you have a large family or you have money. This design is more of the money expression than that of a large family. The round pillars and fenced porch roof strike an immediate classic pose. The shutters add to this. Use of a gabled roof maintains the classic line. Using a hip or other style roof would make this design seem "Stubby".

I doubt George Washington would have placed a two-carriage garage this close to the house, but it is the modern practice. It makes the entire ensemble appear larger. Should you require a garage for a twenty-first century four door pick-up truck, you will definitely need to enlarge this space.

Entering the house we have a half bath to the left. It is at least wheel chair friendly. Ahead is a generous guest closet. To the right there is a rather large great room that could have a gas fireplace installed on the garage wall. Entry from the garage gives a direct path to the kitchen, stairwell, and elevator.

The kitchen is spacious with plenty of room for a breakfast table. If the owner enjoys entertaining, this kitchen location allows isolation of the mundane and sometimes messy food preparation.

This will not be a cheap house to build though no more than a ranch style of equal elegance and accessibility. That elevator adds both utility and luxury to this home. It would be a must for wheel chair access.

On the second floor is a mammoth master bathroom that incorporates both laundry facilities and a real soaking bathtub. To make this space more wheel chair friendly simply reduce the size of the linen closet. The master bedroom is of considerable size and incorporates a large hanging closet. The smaller guest room has an equally large closet. This room would be accessed from the stair well and has direct access to its own three-quarter bath.

Add a third bedroom by construction of either the "Guest Houses" or "The Cottage" would give your guests the most privacy. Adding the "Cottage" would best carry through the Southern Plantation theme?

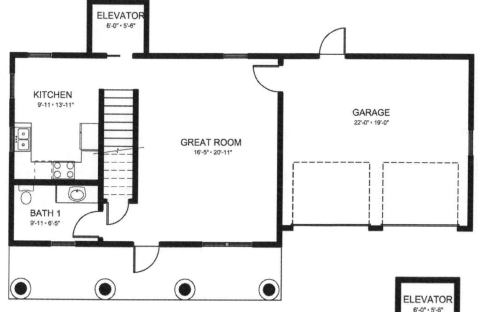

The Theodore

© ℬℕ𝒹𝑒𝓈𝒾𝑔𝓃𝓈

Design # 9-003.003
Heated Square Feet: 1494
Width: 54'- 6"
Depth: 21'- 11"
Bedrooms: 2
Bath: 2.5
Garage: 2 car

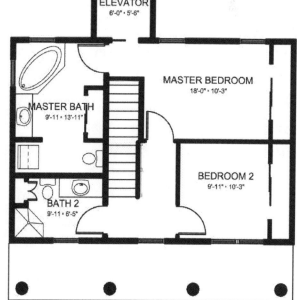

The Salt Box 1

The origin of the salt box goes back to the 16th century England. Although there were one-story dwellings at the time, two-story homes were most common. When a family had growing pains, many found the answer in adding to the back of the house. For sake of simplicity they simply extended the roof from the second floor to the outer wall of the single story addition. Thus the house had a shorter front roof and a much longer rear roof. Looking somewhat like the sloping roof of the salt storage boxes of the time. .

The end-on lay out was often used in later years and is well represented by a house built in Fair View Pennsylvania in 1838. This house known as the Sturgeon house has been placed on the National Register of Historic Places.

In designing the Salt Box, it proved most practical to apply this end-on approach. Thus placing both the garage door and living quarter door on that end. The roof of what would have been the two story section gave ample height for the RV garage. The necessary length of the RV garage, worked out well in creating the living quarters parallel to the garage.

The layout of the living quarters approximates the layout of the 19th century house design best known as a "Shot Gun house". There are still examples of these houses in New Orleans. They were so named because it was said that if you opened the front and back doors and fired a shot gun through the front door, the bullet would not hit anything in the house before exiting through the back door. By turning the living room coat closet 90 degrees we would create the same shot gun path.

The living quarters in this design have everything for comfortable living. From the ample living room through the large eating nook and well equipped galley to the full bath with laundry facilities everything is well placed. The master bedroom has a ten foot long closet and yet has room for a king size bed.

Built on a proper lot, the RV garage will allow one to drive straight-in and straight-out eliminating the dreaded back-up. Finished with stucco and trimmed with a contrasting color it will fit well in the best neighborhood.

This design could serve well for the car collector. Adding two car-park elevators would allow housing up to four cars in the garage. This is something Jay Leno would appreciate. The doors at both ends would make for convenient extraction of the cars. This design has been included with our two-story designs because it is two stories tall, though without a second story.

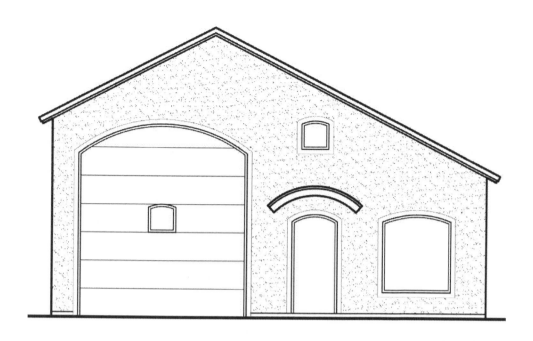

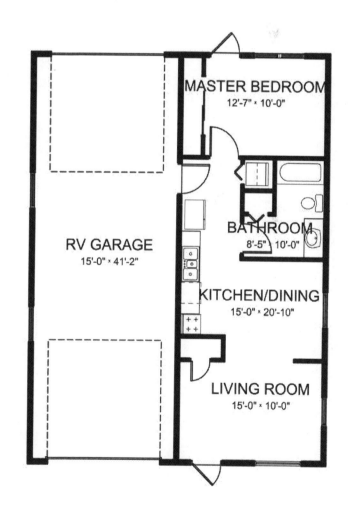

MASTER BEDROOM
12'-7" x 10'-0"

BATHROOM
8'-5" x 10'-0"

RV GARAGE
15'-0" x 41'-2"

KITCHEN/DINING
15'-0" x 20'-10"

LIVING ROOM
15'-0" x 10'-0"

The Salt Box 1

© CNBdesigns

Design # 9-003.007
Heated Square Feet: 681
Width: 31'- 8"
Depth: 42'- 4"
Bedrooms: 1
Bath: 1
Garage: 2 car or 1 RV

The Salt Box 2

The exterior shape of this home is very similar to that of the Salt Box 1, but has an entirely different floor plan. The front of this salt box is usually the side view of a traditional salt box design. The first floor is very similar to our design called The North Star. What sets this design apart is the elevator to the second floor and the somewhat unusual floor plan found there. The entire second floor is actually a large master suite. It is certainly senior friendly.

That day room could be a library, sewing room, a TV / computer room or bunk room for visiting grandchildren. In any event, this suite concept will allow the owners maximum privacy and could afford them a great elevated view.

This particular design has a lot of available storage space. There is a coat closet next to the front door. In the first floor bathroom is an unusually large linen closet. Both bedrooms have good size hanging closets. The master bedroom surely has adequate room to accommodate large his and her dressers. Also on the second floor there is access to storage above the first floor bedroom. Those two closets flanking the stairwell offer additional clothing storage.

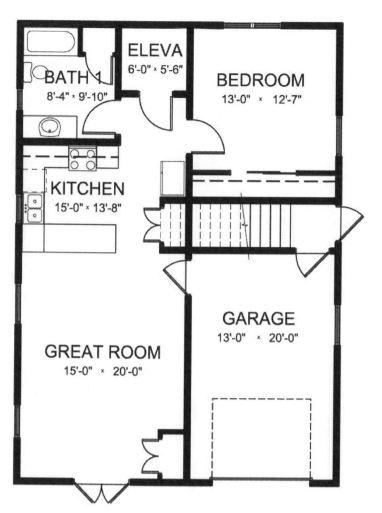

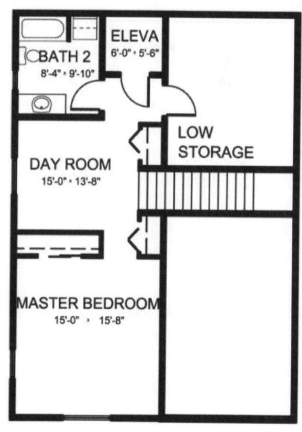

The Salt Box 2

© CNBdesigns

Design # 9-003.008

Heated Square Feet: 1615

Width: 20'- 9"

Depth: 41'- 2"

Bedrooms: 2

Bath: 2

Garage: 1 car

The North Star

It always seems strange to me that one bedroom apartments and studio apartments are looked upon as normal for both those starting out on their own and for seniors in retirement settings. Yet a one bedroom house is considered something less. This one may be a bit unusual, having an included garage. In the 1800s and early 1900s there were lots of homes that were no more than a large one room house with a sleeping loft for the children. We visited an 1800s Volga German house, in the middle of Kansas, that was just such a home. In our early history the entire frontier was dotted with this style home!

The North Star has a generous amount of room and convenience for senior living. It has everything one might find in a three bedroom house, less two of the bedrooms. Some other things this house does not have are larger heat and air conditioning cost, real estate taxes, and more space to clean and dust. In some areas it could be built for as little as $80,000. Over a ten year period the cost would be far less than a similar sized apartment with the garage thrown in as bonus.

That garage is a real worthwhile investment. When it comes time to sell it will make the property more attractive. Not only as a garage but also as a space easily converted to a second bedroom. A new one or two car garage addition could then be constructed on the opposite side of the house. Should a new owner prefer the existing garage. It could be augmented by building a second garage alongside. Then adding a bedroom suite on the opposite side of the house, with the entrance directly into the living room.

This plan is definitely senior friendly. With careful selection of furniture it may even qualify as handicap accessible under some zoning restrictions.

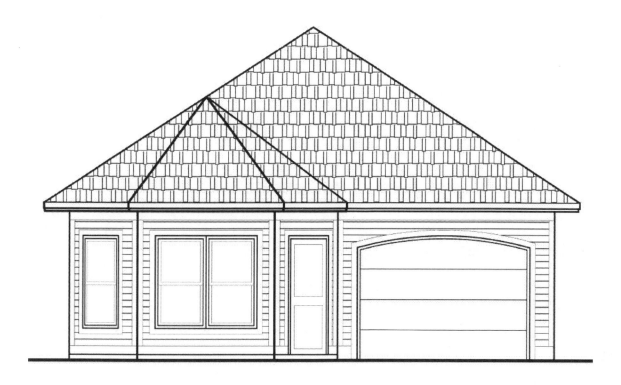

The North Star©

CNBdesigns

Design # 9-003.005
Heated Square Feet: 760
Width: 28'- 8"
Depth: 36'- 9"
Bedrooms: 1
Bath: 1
Garage: 1 car

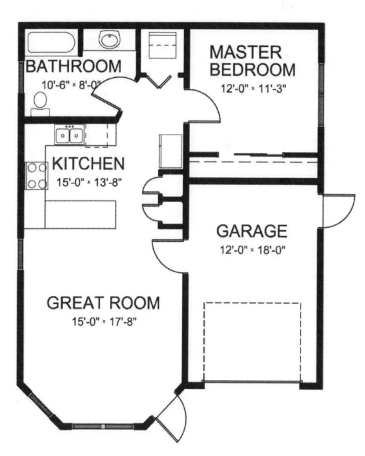

BATHROOM
10'-6" × 8'-0"

MASTER
BEDROOM
12'-0" × 11'-3"

KITCHEN
15'-0" × 13'-8"

GARAGE
12'-0" × 18'-0"

GREAT ROOM
15'-0" × 17'-8"

The Annie

Just think of "Little Orphan Annie. " She is a small place with a wealth of thought spent on her. The idea is more like "LITTLE HOUSE ON THE PRAIRIE "than "THE WALTONS". There is a movement around American campgrounds toward more and more "PARK MODELS. " Annie represents stage two of the Park Model movement. She has the basic dimensions of a stand-alone Park model with the addition of a Florida room (sometimes called an Arizona room.) In this particular case she could be built as a Park Model, Double Wide or as a factory built main unit and an on-site built Florida room. The current practice is for room additions to be built on site.

People who are not familiar with RV floor plans will question the location of the washer and dryer. Ninety-nine percent of one's laundry originates in the bedroom. Forget convention; wash it where you drop it. There are some real advantages to this. You do not have to carry it to another room and back. Many people living in small homes have to carry laundry to the car, drive to the Laundromat, and then reverse the process. The $20 or more you would spend each week on this process, will very quickly pay for all the laundry equipment needed. When your clothing comes out of the dryer it can immediately be hung in the closet or folded and put in a drawer. Should you want to hang your clothes on a line to dry, there is an exit door to step out of right there. You could string a clothes line right outside the door and it would not be visible from the front of the house. One of those umbrella clothes line units would be perfect in the court yard or on the deck.

Many people moving from a larger living arrangement find most Park Models lacking in storage space. This particular plan has considerable storage in both the kitchen and dining room. The dining room side of the bathroom wall has room for a wall-length hutch. There will remain a large dining space. With an expandable dining table you could accommodate as many as eight people for Thanksgiving.

The Florida room could be set up conversation pit style, while providing excellent TV viewing. The settee could convert to a guest bed. The deck outside will accommodate a porch swing or a couple of deck chairs. It is recommended that a retractable awning be installed to cover the entire deck area. Be it mountain, shore, or desert home, this small house will be comfortable for a retiring couple or a great getaway cottage.

The Annie

© CNBdesigns

Design # 9-003.015
Heated Square Feet: 612
Width: 24'- 0"
Depth: 35'- 4"
Bedrooms: 1
Bath: 1

MASTER BEDROOM
11'-1" × 8'-6"

BATH
7'-7" × 6'-4"

DINING
7'-10" × 8'-6"

GREAT ROOM
11'6" × 14'-10"

KITCHEN
11'-1" × 7'-0"

The Guest House 1

The Guest House is basically an on-site motel-style accommodation for two. There is provision for a small but full service kitchen without a dishwasher. When the Guest House is used as a studio this feature will certainly be handy. The bay front gives this design its own "personality." A Murphy wall-bed will make this living space very versatile and could even be comfortable for extended periods. The porch / carport is definitely a handy asset and could be constructed as an enclosed garage.

The Guest House 2

This design is much like the original Guest House with the addition of a separate bedroom. This addition makes for a much more comfortable and longer term housing accommodation.

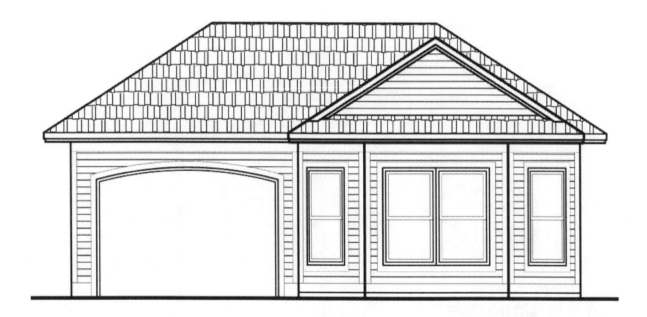

The Guest House 1

© CNBdesigns

Design # 9-003.006.1
Heated Square Feet: 381
Width: 28'- 9"
Depth: 24'- 9"
Bedrooms: 1
Bath: 1

PORCH / CARPORT
12'-0" × 20'-0"

BATHROOM
15'-0" × 5'-5"

GREAT ROOM / STUDIO
15'-0" × 17'-9"

The Guest House 2

© CNBdesigns

Design # 9-003.006.2
Heated Square Feet: 525
Width: 20'- 9"
Depth: 42'- 2"
Bedrooms: 1
Bath: 1

PORCH / CARPORT
12'-0" × 30'-0"

BATHROOM
15'-0" × 5'-5"

BEDROOM
15'-0" × 12'-7"

GREAT ROOM
15'-0" × 13'-6"

The Cottage 1 & 2

These two plans share design ideas with the Guest House 1 and Guest house 2. The major difference is the frontal orientation; the Cottage has its long side as the front while the Guest House is end-on. The Cottage series gains usable square footage by having squared ends all-round. Like the Guest House the basic Cottage is little more than a motel accommodation. The Cottage 2 bedroom version has slightly more privacy due to the placement of the bath between it and the great room. This design also favors the great room with larger usable square footage area.

The Cottage 1

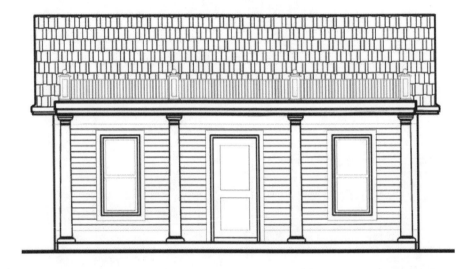

The Cottage 1

© CNBdesigns

Design # 9-003.009
Heated Square Feet: 395
Width: 28'- 9"
Depth: 24'- 9"
Bedrooms: 1
Bath: 1

BATHROOM
5'-5" × 15'-0"

PORCH /
CARPORT
12'-7" × 21'-2"

STUDIO
15'-0" × 17'-9"

The Cottage 2

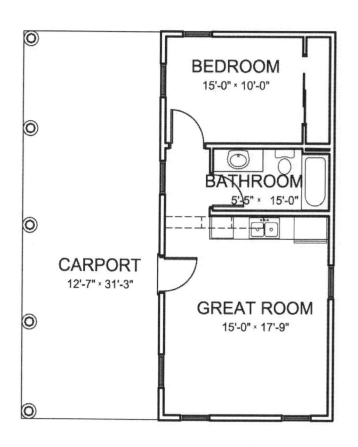

BEDROOM
15'-0" × 10'-0"

BATHROOM
5'-5" × 15'-0"

CARPORT
12'-7" × 31'-3"

GREAT ROOM
15'-0" × 17'-9"

The Cottage 2
© CNBdesigns

Design # 9-003.010
Heated Square Feet: 557
Width: 20'- 9"
Depth: 42'- 2"
Bedrooms: 1
Bath: 1

Introduction to Park Model Homes

What is a Park Model Home? In all states except Florida, a Park Model Home is a recreational park trailer built to the American National Standards Institute (ANSI) 119.5 code. It must have a floor plan having less than 400 square feet and has its axles and wheels attached. This is actually measured using the outside dimensions of the living area. Lofts and covered porches are not subjected to the same limitations. Lofts may not exceed one half the area of the basic unit. Porches at either end or both ends add a lot of living space. They could have roll up canvas walls with plastic windows for wind protection in addition to screening. In Florida, they allow floor plans up to 499 square feet. For the 399 square foot class, the most popular models are roughly 11 feet by 35 feet. These units do require special permits to move down the road. They do not require chase cars or lead cars. Park models are taxed as RVs rather than as real property.

A Park Model can be placed anywhere allowable by local zoning laws, not just in an RV park or mobile home park. There is no reason that a group of them can't form their own little community. Think of them as cottages with or without the white picket fence. More and more seniors are looking for affordable places to live. Most Park Models are built much better than the older mobile homes. Many have metal roofs and fiber-cement siding, which makes their exterior fire resistant.

Most manufacturers will work with customers. While some work exclusively through dealers others will work factory direct. In any event, Park Model Homes deserve a serious look by those seeking a great place to live at a more affordable price. You can have almost anything in a Park Model that you can have in a custom built house.

Most Park Model units will not have water pumps, water tanks or waste tanks. They will be plumbed much like a site-built home. The one thing most needed in a small home is STORAGE. When choosing a floor plan keep this in mind. I strongly recommend visiting many dealers and as many manufacturers as possible.

Do not get caught up in the old real estate cliché: "It shows well" or "It has curb appeal." Obviously you don't want ugly, but you can have both an attractive home and a well thought out workable floor plan. It would be prudent to start a list of features you want in your home. Take a copy with you each time you visit a dealer or manufacturer. Check off each item you find on your list and add items you realize you hadn't thought about, but find desirable. Be sure to note the make and model. A good idea might be to grade each model on its storage area. Your first walk through will give you an idea as to how much you like the floor plan. If it really appeals to you, go back through with a tape measure in hand. Make a spread sheet showing width of hanging wardrobe space, bedroom drawer space, kitchen cupboard and drawer space. Should you find a floor plan you particularly like in a catalogue, contact the maker. Request a floor plan marked with the actual dimensions and number of storage areas. Example: 10 Drawers 18" wide by 12" deep, 2 hanging wardrobes 24" X 30" deep. After you have checked out a few models, you can then compare them for the best storage. This will help you narrow your choices. Most makers will allow options or small changes but don't really want to "start from scratch!" In the end, be sure to personally inspect the model you are going to buy.

Park Model homes come in a variety of trim levels. Some will come with solid wood cabinet doors and drawers but low-cost models will have vinyl covered cabinet sides etc. Solid wood cabinets are far superior to the vinyl covered. While the vinyl models may be well made for what they are, they may not endure the bumps and knocks of full-time living. Another drawback is color change. Even solid wood doors will have a color shift over time. The vinyl covered panels will also have color change. The two materials when new will be quite comparable, but after a couple of years they will be less comparable as their color changes at different rates. Recommendation: budget and availability considerations permitting, choose the solid wood cabinets.

Counter tops and sinks are also a good place to option-up. A bathroom solid surface counter top with molded sink will look great for many years. (Ours is over 10 years old and looks like new) Plastic sinks on cheap laminate, not-so-much. Kitchen counter tops made of high quality laminate or solid surface counter tops should look good for many years. Things happen in the kitchen, so I recommend top mounted stainless steel sinks. They are tough and easy to replace if damaged. Conversely, they are easy to reuse should the counter top be damaged or the cook simply wants a different look. Stainless is also good in the bathroom, though not so homey there.

Most all manufacturers offer "LOFT" models that have very limited head-room in the loft area. These are sufficient only for small children, or as a sleeping loft. These lofts can be used as storage areas. If you plan on locating in an area that experiences heavy snow falls, the almost flat roof of a loft model may not be strong enough for the snow load of the region. On the other hand, if the area of the loft roof is kept small it should have the strength to handle reasonable snow loads.

Know the insulation factors of all models that appeal to you. Remember insulation is important for BOTH heat and air-conditioning. Some makers offer up-grades here too. I cannot stress enough the importance of both quality construction and the use of quality materials.

One item often over-looked, is commonly known as "Hurricane Straps." These are metal straps firmly attached to the basic framework of a unit and attached to ground anchors. No matter where your Park Model is to be located these should be on your must have list. These are included in the ANSI code.

Consider adding a smaller Park Model next to the main Park Model, as a guest-house. This unit might only have a bathroom and bedroom but provide motel-like accommodations for your guests or a "Dog House" for an errant spouse!

I am including floor plans from two manufacturers. I have visited both facilities and would recommend them as sources. Also included will be a few idea plans, not currently being built by any manufacturer.

Athens Park Homes

Athens, Texas is south east of Dallas on US Route 175. Athens Park Homes are built here and sent all over the Southwest. They will actually deliver them anywhere you want. They have developed an amazing number of floor plans. Surely one of them will fit your dreams. This company actually assembles and welds their trailer chassis in a 17,000 square foot frame shop.

Athens homes standard exterior includes fiber-cement siding by James Hardie. Optional log or cedar siding is also popular. Flooring is of thick tongue and groove plywood or OSB. Standard interior walls and ceilings are drywall, finished with tape, textured and have rounded corners for a smooth finished look. Knotty pine is an option here. The built-in cabinetry is well done.

I especially like the bay window dresser in the bedroom shown in the attached floor plan. The only change I would make to this plan would be to add an access sliding door (bed side) to the storage space located between the bed and the washer / dryer. As a hanging closet this could be loaded right from the dryer and accessed for dressing from the bedroom.

Not everyone will go for the galley kitchen of the plan shown here. They do offer a variety of other kitchen layouts. Their brochure presents no less than six loft models, based on some of their best floor plans. In the case of the model 201 shown here, it becomes the model 201 with a loft by simply replacing that closet mentioned above with a stairway to the storage / sleeping loft above.

All indications are that ATHENS PARK HOMES will be a great company to work with.

Champion Home Builders, a giant in the industry, recently purchased Athens Park Homes. The Athens Park Homes will soon be available from manufacturing plants in Weiser, ID; Lindsay, CA; Chandler, AZ; York, NE; Sanger Field, NY; Salisbury, NC; Lake City, FL; and of course Athens, TX.

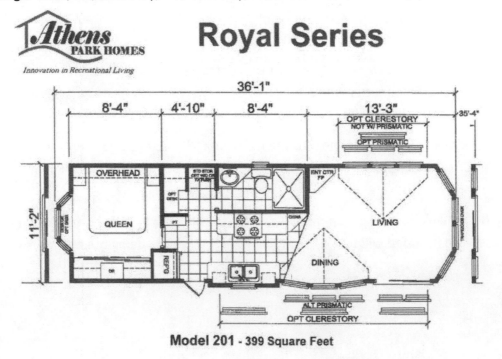

Model 201 - 399 Square Feet

Pinnacle Park Model Homes

Pinnacle Park Homes are built at Ochlocknee in Southwest Georgia. This family owned business is quite impressive, I actually saw the president of the company running a floor sander on a unit during production. That is what I call hands-on management!

They build a wide variety of floor plans and have even built one on pontoons for a customer who really wanted waterfront living. I guess you can't say they have a standard floor plan because they have so many different floor plans. The larger models measure 11 feet by 35 feet. A very good percentage of their production has cedar siding with natural finish interiors. Also available are vinyl siding, split Log siding and fiber-cement siding. Interiors can have an optional vinyl covered dry wall. Those knotty pine cabinets are solid wood. If you do not like knotty pine there are other choices. You can top this all with either a metal roof or architectural shingles.

They will build you a fine Park Model and have several smaller models you could park next door to accommodate family or friends when they come to visit.

The floor plan shown has excellent space usage with enough openness to make it seem like a larger home.

Got a special idea for your park model home? Ask Pinnacle? You may be pleasantly surprised just how versatile this small homebuilder can be.

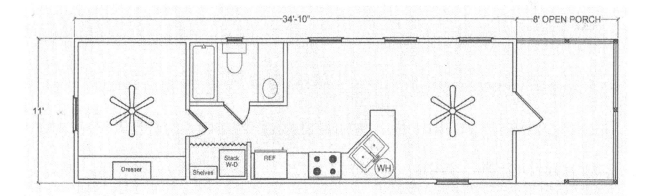

The Maxi Park

This Taylor / BNB design measures eleven feet wide and thirty six feet long. The Maxi Park Model has 396 square of living floor plan. It is dubbed the "Maxi" because it has a tremendous amount of storage and easy access room. Starting in the bedroom, we find a closet that runs the width of the unit and is over ten feet long by two feet in depth. The total height of the closet is six feet six inches, allowing for installing two hang rods one above the other. This would permit doubling the shirt hanging in at least a portion of the closet. Another option would be shoe racks below the hanging rod. A dresser measuring almost nine feet in length with over cabinet lies across from a queen sized bed. Unusually wide aisles run on each side of the bed with nicely-sized night stands at the head of the bed.

The walk-through bathroom has privacy pocket doors at each end. It would be possible to park a wheel chair alongside the toilet and access the sink. The shower is also large enough for a seat and handicap rails. Front loading laundry equipment would also allow wheel chair access.

Entering the great room from the bath area, we find a coat closet across from the main entry. Next to the closet is space for a love seat or two recliners across from a large flat screen TV. Next to the TV is the refrigerator, followed by twelve feet of L-shaped counter containing a double sink and a cooktop. A micro wave / convection oven can be installed above or below the cooktop. Installing it below will allow wheel chair access. There is a dining table for two that is expandable to seat four next to a picture window.

This unit has vaulted ceilings from the kitchen to the bedroom. There is a storage loft above the bedroom still allowing for six foot six inches of head-room in the bedroom. It would be a good hiding place for Christmas presents or stowing things that are seldom used.

The Ruby Jane

The Ruby Jane is the smallest park model in our series of homes / cottages. She has a remarkably comfortable living space for her small size. The trick of course is that the Murphy style bed has a dining table hinged to its underside. During the day when the bed is closed and in an upright position the table drops down for use.

Even with so small a space, options can be applied to individualize this home. This design will allow the instillation of a corner gas log fireplace. With proper instillation you could still have your TV above it. Careful selection of the fire place will make it possible to heat this cozy little home while enjoying a romantic fire.

That porch is deep enough to allow the installation of a two person porch swing at one side and a couple of deck chairs at the other side. The porch would be best served with a fixed roof.

While we are looking at possible options, consider building this unit with a fold-up front porch and a retractable awning. That porch could be folded up against the front of the house exposing the trailer hitch. Retract the awning, disconnect the utilities and it's ready to tow down the road. OK, you should probably secure everything inside. Yes, it would require wide load permits and is not something you would want to do every month. When and if you move a Park Model, remember to reattach the hurricane-straps to ground anchors.

All Park Models are able to be relocated. One Park Model Manufacturer said they were amazed at the number of their units that had been moved great distances by the second owners. There are other reasons to move a Park Model, like "There Goes the Neighborhood!" New owners may not keep up the park as well as the first owners or increase the rent. Then there is the possibility you get new neighbors that are loud and obnoxious! Maybe you just decide you would like to try Arizona after a few years in Florida.

Those people lucky enough to live on larger acreage could use a unit like this to house an aging but self-sufficient parent. They would be near enough at hand to assist as needed but could still have their independence. Zoning laws would have to be observed. In most places such a unit on private property would not cause additional property tax liability.

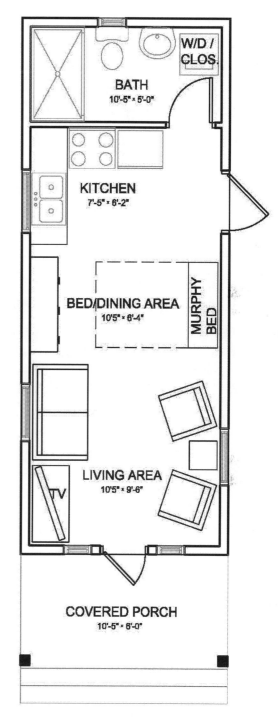

The Ruby Jane

© ℬℕℬdesigns

Design # 9-003.201
Heated Square Feet: 319
Width: 11'- 4"
Depth: 34'- 2" w/ Porch
Bedrooms: 1
Bath: 1

The Tiny House Movement

Google "TINY HOUSE" and you will find an amazing number of Tiny House designs. There are also blogs and You Tube entries proclaiming the many advantages of living small. This book would not be complete without some consideration of this trend. Many of the tiny houses presented online are really small Park Models that can be towed down the road without special permits, by a pick-up or larger SUV. Regular house siding, pitched roofs, porches and normal house plumbing, set these "cottages" apart from the average travel trailer.

A lot has been written about building your own Tiny House. Some claim you can build your own house for about half the cost of a similar commercial built unit. Building costs will vary greatly and are highly dependent on the resourcefulness and skills of the builder. Buying odd lots, cut-offs, and clearance items can help keep construction costs down. It is also possible to achieve significant savings by acquiring slightly used components. One of the best reasons for building one of these yourself, is that you can insure the quality of the components and materials.

I have prepared a floor plan for a slightly larger "Tiny House" shown on the following page and named the Hunter. Let's look at the individual components of this design and the reasons behind their inclusion. The centrally located entry door divides this unit into two distinct areas. To the right is a good-sized entertainment and conversation area. Next to that, is a dinette table that drops down when the wall bed is in the closed position. Those chairs seen in the conversation area will double as dining chairs. There are cabinets marked ST for storage. These can be specified to contain drawers, doors or serve as hanging lockers. The one next to the refrigerator (marked REF) can even be a desk with drawers on one or both sides. All these can have overhead cabinets installed above them.

The TV in the entertainment / conversation area can be viewed from the love seat across the room. For a special show, such as the Super Bowl, those two chairs can be repositioned in a semi-circle with the love seat. If mounted on plywood and hinged it can be swung out for better viewing from the bed.

The inclusion of a wall-bed helps make this tiny house seem far more spacious than it would otherwise. Its position allows access from both sides for both entry and ease in making it up. Many tiny houses only have "loft beds" or ones with limited access and are difficult to enter and even more difficult to make up.

The rather large bathroom contains space for a wardrobe or washer dryer, shower, sink, and toilet. This design requires full campground hook-ups, including electric, water, and sewer.

Want to make this unit self-contained? Install a composting toilet, a gray water tank, water supply tank and a water pump. Some locations suitable for this unit may actually allow release of "gray water" to the ground.

To complete the idea of this tiny house being more like a cottage than a trailer the hitch can be fabricated to be removable. Removal of the tires and installation of a full skirt will further this image.

This unit is configured to allow owner transport from campground to campground. You could spend your summer in the mountains, or on a northern lake. Come winter, a move to Florida or the South West would be in order. This design readily lends itself to owner construction.

The Hunter

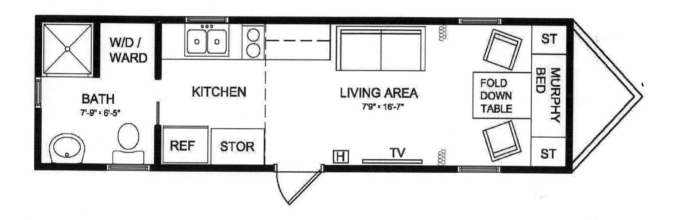

The Hunter

© CNBdesigns

Design # 9-003.301
Heated Square Feet: 252
Width: 8'- 4"
Depth: 30'- 3" Plus hitch
Bedrooms: 1
Bath: 1

Be an Energy Miser

Be an energy miser; use the least energy necessary to accomplish any task. This is incremental power usage. A good example of this is my entertainment center, consisting of a TV – DVD-satellite receiver, antenna amplifier and stereo. In my home, each of these units has its own power switch. When watching a DVD, only the TV and DVD player are using any power. Okay, I hear you: You have three remotes and now I want you to have to throw in a bunch of switches – Damn! If you still want to live rich and have money for toys, you should seriously consider participating in incremental power usage to save money. Every appliance you own that has a light on it that glows when the appliance is turned off, is eating a small amount of power. Some that don't have that light are still having a snack on electric at your expense. There is a little device called a Kill a Watt 4400 you can use to discover the actual power usage of any 120-volt appliance both on and off! This little device will help you become an energy miser. In 2008 I bought one for under $30. You can get one through the internet at www.p3international.com or Camping World and now some home supply stores carry these or similar devices.

At present (2013) LEDS hold much promise, but are costly. LEDS require direct current (DC.) Because all America, and most of the world, is hard wired for alternating current (AC) electric power, moving to DC power will require some serious changes for existing structures. LED light bulbs with built in AC to DC conversion can help bridge that gap. With good planning new construction can be designed to avoid these problems. In the meantime replacing old light bulbs with LED converted bulbs will give savings long term.

Putting lights only where needed will also reduce the wattage needed and power consumption. Don't try to use a ceiling light for reading. An LED reading light next to your Lazy Boy will provide all the light you will need. Take a hard look at your furniture arrangement. You don't need to light up a room like Las Vegas just to watch TV!

Now that we have a grasp of the incremental lighting concept, how do we make it work for us? First, we must learn to turn off lights. This will be really hard for some. Think of electric in other terms. Electricity, like money, can only be spent once. Use too much unnecessary electric and you will have to buy more, produce more and/or store more. In the case of a solar powered system you will need more storage batteries and more solar panels, at least!

Selecting Appliances and Other Stuff

Let's face it; we all have prejudices about brand names. Some like GE, Whirlpool or some other brand. I think this one is best, you think that one is best. Brand preference is not bad. It shows you care and may have had a good experience with that brand. Don't stop there. You haven't been a good shopper if you don't research at least three brands of each appliance. Once it is bought, and installed, you own it. No turning back. Be smart and be happy and don't have to return the product with a lame excuse. A lot of companies are cracking down on their return policy. You might just get stuck. Sometimes there will be a restocking charge. OUCH!

To avoid getting the wrong appliance, make a check list for each type of appliance. Such a check list might look something like this:

Refrigerator

Brand	Source	Location	Capacity	Dimensions	Energy	Warranty	Service
GE	Lowes	Main St.	18 FT	68Hx30Wx30D	60 watts	2yrs	Local

Measure, measure, measure, I can speak from experience. You can't get a 15 cu. ft. refrigerator in a 12 cu. ft. space. If the space is made for a specific size, the super capacity will not fit. So you will be wasting your time because you failed to measure.

Getting the product features you want is paramount. Should you get a front load washer or top load? Two years down the road is too late to make that decision. If you want the front load, ask and ask again to find out if it is available. Some sales people only want to sell what is in stock or what has the highest commission.

Don't drive 30 miles or more to save $5.00. Remember, if there is a problem you will have to drive 30 miles back just to see that dealer. I would suggest a 20 mile limit unless you can get 25% to 30% price reduction. You should think long and hard about those extended warranties. It must be a cost verses benefit decision. We have sometimes elected to buy an extended warranty and it paid off. Other times were different. We always tried to evaluate the cost of repairs and chances of break downs. On one occasion we had an extended warranty on our washing machine and it paid off. The two service repair visits exceeded the cost of the warranty. Remember, these are insurance policies and it is easy to be insurance poor. Sometimes you need to carry the risk yourself.

Another source of an extended warranty is your credit card company. Check each of your credit cards to see if they offer a one year extension on purchases made with their card. This will not be true of all card companies and each will have specific rules as to coverage. It has worked for us. If it is available with one of your credit cards, it is a NO COST benefit. Use it on all large purchases even if you could pay cash!

In all your purchases remember service expenses. Remember also, doing it yourself is worth 120% of the service charge. Simply put, you save the service charge, the sales tax, and the income tax you would have had to pay using your earned dollars.

Allocate your funds to live small but live rich. Enjoy the best and pay the least. Do you think the rich have always paid top dollar? Only when showing off. You don't get rich by "giving" your money to others. Think of all this money saving as a game. It's you against the world. It's you against the retailer. That is how the sales people think.

Have you ever had fun buying a new car? I mean in addition to the joy of getting that special car with that great "new car smell." I have. A few years back, I arranged with my credit union to have an open ended car loan, with a predetermined term. They sent a check requiring me to fill in the amount and sign after calling them for approval. Then the fun began!! I'm sure you have experienced the typical car sales ploy of having the sales person "check" with their sales manager.   I countered this by showing them I had the check and was ready to deal. So off he went to ok the deal with the sales manager. He came back with a slightly different deal. I excused myself to go talk with my banker, by cell phone. Then I too returned with a new and different deal. I was actually talking to my credit union. There is actually some question in my mind as to what actually goes on in those sales manager conferences. Are they really trying to give me a good deal or having a smoke and coffee? While letting me stew over the deal to soften me up for an ever so slightly different deal.

The worst car deal I was ever involved with included the salesman trying to hold the keys to the customers' car hostage until he accepted the latest deal. The lesson here is to remember: if there is anything bothering you, about a purchase, you should WALK AWAY!! Sometimes just the act of walking away can make the seller see it your way.

 Your actions can have unintended consequences. Pushing that deal beyond reason can come back to haunt you. Let's take a case in which you cut the salesman's commission from $1000 to $100. When returning to that dealer for service your sales person can work for you. If you actually beat them badly they may only half-heartedly represent you with the service department.

Always ask about discounts and sales terms. Will they honor price drops within 30 days? On larger expenditures shop at least three dealers, search the internet, and check local advertising media. Be prepared with plan "B". Know the dealers inventory as much as you can. Is there a different color or model with fewer options in inventory that you could accept if the price were right? You can use the old bait and switch routine in reverse. Remember the fancier higher priced item usually has a greater mark-up. There are two ways to make this work for you. First, decide how much you are willing to pay for an item you want. Second, how much would you pay for an alternative choice? Then a trip to each of three dealers with note pad, will give you a good starting point. Then comes what I call Dickering Up and Dickering Down. Dickering Up is negotiating price on a mid-line product and going below what you feel the sales person will accept. Let us say your research shows a really good sale price is 40% of current retail. Offer 45% off retail. See just how low they will go. Stick to your price. One of two things will happen, they will not meet your price or they will. You can respond to either of these actions the same way just using different words. If they don't meet your price simply switch to the top of the line and make an offer at 45% of list price. Should they meet your price on the lesser unit but you would rather have the top of the line simply say, "I can see you aren't really comfortable with the deal." Then make an offer on the top of the line at 45% off retail. Dickering Down works just the opposite in that you start with negotiating on the top of the line and then make an offer to purchase the mid-line at a deep discount.

The most important thing is prepare yourself for getting the most for your money. KNOW THE MARKET and KNOW YOUR PRICES!!! That computer price advertised in the Sunday Flyer may really be for a model lacking features and brought in only as a sales gimmick. There is one company that is forever having "Door Busting Sales." If a company is always having "Sales" their regular prices may be bogus and so may be their sales price! You must know the prices offered by other outlets.

Keep this in mind: Buying food at a higher price because you are hungry and it's the only food in town is one thing. Buying a new anything at an inflated price when you could do better is just plain stupid. Take the emotion out of your shopping. Finding out you just gave some slick salesman $100 more than you should have may not make for a pleasant evening with your spouse!

I can't say often enough, "KNOW YOUR PRICES," check the competition, and offer a lower amount! These days you hear politicians say they want you to keep more of your money. The car dealer or the appliance salesman doesn't feel that way. I don't care if you are 5 foot 2 and only 95 pounds. You can go toe to toe with that 6 foot 4 salesman and win! Just stick to your guns and remember he needs you, the customer, more than you need him!

Power for Living OFF the GRID

The cost of having electrical power brought into remote areas can be daunting. It could cost several thousand dollars. Having your own system at a similar or even lesser cost is definitely an attractive option. No matter what your final primary source of power will be, you should have some sort of generator (gas or diesel). Start your planning with a generator. Size your generator to supply all of your needs, including air-conditioning, if desired. A solar power system can be added later to augment the generator system and save fuel dollars.

Motor homes generally come with some sort of built-in generator and charging system. For travel trailers, 5th wheels and all others there are several stand-alone generator and charger / inverters available. It is highly recommended that the generator have a minimum of 2000 watts of power and the inverter / charger should have a minimum of 40 charging amps and 1000 watts of power at 120v. Combination units are highly recommended for ease of installation and automatic control. Saving money here could be a mistake. Remember the saying "Buy Cheap, Buy Twice." Square wave inverters are usually much cheaper than sine wave inverters. A sine wave inverter actually produces 120 volts of power that is cleaner than that produced by many commercial power generators. This "clean" power will treat all your sophisticated electronic equipment with kid gloves. If your motor home came with a square wave inverter you could consider isolating those circuits used by TV, and computer etc. and feeding them off a separate, small sine wave inverter.

Let's look at a hypothetical inexpensive base line system. This system will not run an air-conditioner but would run a washer but not a dryer. Starting with a generator:

 # 1 A 2000 Watt Honda or its equivalent

 #2 An inverter / charger such as a Magnum Energy 1000 watt inverter with 50 amp charger or equal

  #3 Deep cycle batteries with at least a total power rating of about 400 amps at 12 volts

 A voltage meter or other battery condition meter should be mounted in a convenient location to monitor the charge level of your batteries. Remember it is best not to discharge below 12.2v.

This system will provide sufficient battery power for modest lighting including a TV, a satellite receiver, and a laptop computer. The generator will also provide power for a microwave (direct connect.) A four to six battery system will also provide power to run an RV furnace at lower temperatures while you sleep. To insure the best performance from this or any off-grid system, it is necessary to observe all economy of usage practices.

After some experience with a system like this, you will be able to determine your needs for solar panels.

Solar Power

To understand solar power we first need to discuss what components make up a solar power system. Obviously, the first component must be some sort of receptor that will receive energy from the sun and convert it into a usable form. The simplest illustration of a receptor would be a garden hose lying in the sun on a hot summer afternoon. Even if this hose has good reflective qualities it will absorb the heat of the sun and transfer it to the water inside of the hose. To make this more efficient, we would use a black hose since the color black is known to have the best radiant energy absorbance. Using a coil or zigzag hose pattern and entrapping it in a black box with a clear glass on the top would give us a fairly good model of a solar collector. That glass cover helps trap the suns heat and insulates the hose from the effects of cool air flowing over the solar collector. This would demonstrate a hydro-solar panel.

To best use the energy (heat) generated by this system, you will need both an insulated storage tank and a circulation pump. Unless you are heating water for a dishwasher, you will only need water at about 100 to 105 degrees. Most household systems today heat water to 140 degrees to accommodate the dishwasher. Most small families run a dishwasher once a day. If attached to commercial power or other high capacity power source, you could have an auxiliary water heater run just before dish washing.

For a simple example, a system would include a low volume water pump (probably 12 volt) tubing to connect to the hydro-solar panel and a hot water storage tank. The best type of water heater for this purpose would be similar to that used on boats which uses the engine hot water to heat tank water. In a system of this kind, the water from the hydro-solar heater would never actually touch the water in the storage tank, and should contain anti-freeze. I only mention this as a way to show how simply solar energy can be harnessed for useful purposes. This simple water heating systems described above, can be a good do-it-yourself project.

The more popular solar systems use photocells to convert the suns' rays directly into electrical current. The current product is direct current, usually referred to as DC current. DC current flows from a positive terminal to a negative terminal just like your car battery. Appliances requiring direct current (DC) are growing in numbers as we move toward a greater and greater dependence on electronic devices.

Too often people are over-whelmed with the complexity and cost of solar energy. What you need is a STEPPED PLAN. Make a list of all those things you would like to power with solar energy to save money. Usually the first and easiest will be lighting, second would be all the general purpose outlets. I do not recommend an air-conditioner or any heating element be solar powered, unless you have multi megawatts of power available. For most people, their first venture into alternative power needs to be limited so they can see what it will do for them.

To apply a STEPPED PLAN in a well-organized manner you need to consider your end goal first. Calculate the power required for the maximum usage you want. Make an appliance check list for all electronic devices you are expecting to install. Add extra ones you might decide on later, but have not yet acquired. Divide your list into incremental portions by the amount of power consumption.   That is: lighting, refrigerator, elevator, microwave, TV, and stereo system, etc. Now prioritize from a safety first stand point.

This is how my list would look:

1 Lighting

2 General-purpose outlets including the TV

3 Refrigerator

4 Microwave

Notice that heating, air conditioning, and an electric stove are missing from this list. These items simply require a lot of electricity and are impractical in a small system. The refrigerator may also fall into this category.

Calculate the wattage required by each group. The total wattage will determine the battery storage required to supply your needs. It will also be the indicator of what you will require from an inverter. The inverter is an electronic device used to change DC current to the AC current. Most household appliances commonly use AC current. Today's solar panels produce only DC current. All LED lighting and other LED electronics, such as LED TVs, require DC power. Most LED TVs, and laptop computers will come with a small electrical converter. This small "black box" will convert regular house current to the DC required.

Keep in mind if your source of power is a 12- volt system, you must have ten amps at 12 volts for every one amp at 120 volts. A 120-watt LCD TV that uses one amp at 120v will require 10 amps at 12v! If your system will provide 200 amps, you will be able to watch TV for 20 hrs. Only if you do it in the dark! A 42-inch screen uses about 217 watts at 120 volts. It's about 1.8 amps at 120 volts and whopping 18 amps on a 12-volt circuit. When reading the electrical specification label on an appliance remember:

Volts X Amps = Watts and Watts divided by Volts = Amps. Watts therefore is a derived number. It is commonly used to compare appliance power consumption. For our purposes AMPS (amperage) is the most important number.

Think of an AMP as a gallon of gas. If your tank holds 10 gallons and you only get 10 miles per gallon you will only have a 100-mile range. Battery manufacturers, generator makers and some appliance makers label their products with the amperage information. Most battery condition meters and volt meters tell only the current voltage of the **battery** but this is a good indicator of battery charge. As the battery voltage drops so does the available amperage. Some meters are sophisticated and read out percentage of battery power remaining. The attempt here is not to make you an electrician, but to give you some basic knowledge that will enable you to understand those labels on appliances and other equipment.

Looking at a battery system claiming to have 400 amps, we need to recognize that draining a battery will drastically reduce the life of the battery. To realize maximum battery life, do not use more than one half of the amperage available. For the various types of lead acid batteries it means not discharging below 12.2 volts. If you can afford those hi-tech Lithium batteries, follow the manufacturer's recommendations.

For most families the TV will be used the greatest number of continuous hours per day, compared to any other appliance. I am so old I can actually remember when a 25-inch screen was max then came the 27-inch screen and the rush to "mine's bigger than yours! " Some people will never be happy, even when the people on the screen are actually life size. The problem with these huge screen TVs is that you need a really big room, and they eat power. A 42-inch TV will use 200 watts plus and will be overwhelming in the average size room. On the other hand, a modern 26 to 32 inch flat screen LED TV will use about 30 to 80 watts of power and be at home in a room as small as 10 X 12 ft. That room costs less to build, has lower taxes applied, and is cheaper to heat and air condition. This is a big savings and helps to achieve "Living Rich on a Small Income."

 A basic system designed to supply power to all household lighting, computing power, and TV, would be about 400 watts of solar panels, a 40 amp controller, four 6v golf cart batteries, and an inverter / charger of 1000 – 2000 watts. Golf cart batteries are normally rated at six volts and must be hooked together in series pairs to form a 12-volt power source. Hooking two or more such pairs together in parallel will result in a 12-volt battery bank. To hook in series means to connect the positive of one battery to the negative of the second. This will leave one positive terminal on one battery not yet hooked to anything. The other battery will have a negative not connected. These terminals become the positive and negative of a resulting 12-volt power source. You can hook as many pairs together in parallel (positive to positive and negative to negative) as you like, and still have only a 12-volt DC power bank. The advantage to this is that each pair added will increase the amp hours available, extending the amount of available energy. This set-up of 400 watts solar and 400 amps of battery power should provide you with enough electric power for your LED lighting needs and about four hours of TV viewing, plus charge your computer. Of course you must observe all the requirements of economizing stated earlier.

There is one exception to the no heating element rule mentioned earlier. We have a 12- volt crockpot purchased at a truck stop. While only six inches across and about 4 inches deep, it will cook a meal for two in about four hours. We employ it on sunny days after our solar panels have fully charged our batteries. Full charge is usually achieved by noon. During the afternoon the solar panels replace the power consumed by the crockpot. This could be considered "Solar Cooking." This is one example of "an exception to the rule."

 For further reading on this subject I recommend, "MANAGING ON 12 VOLTS," by Harold Barre

Living on the Road

 Examination of history would indicate that Gypsies were probably the earliest "RVers." Their name "Gypsy" is derived from the country name Egypt; however the Gypsies probably originated in India or at least that area. They may have been thought to be from Egypt due to their darker skin. In any event, these nomadic people built and lived in very fancy wagons drawn by horses. From these caravans they plied their trades of handyman, carpenter, and fortune teller.   Because of their seeming carefree and nomadic life-style they were often viewed as unreliable and dishonest with a criminal bent. The Gypsy movement spread to Western Europe and Great Britain. In Scotland they were known as "Tinkers" and definitely looked upon as untrustworthy. The exact timing of their arrival in America is not known. But arrive they did. Their reputation followed them and they were not warmly received.

While the Gypsies were often looked down upon, some people actually envied their carefree life-style. In the late 1800s rich Britons sought out and bought some of the very ornate Gypsy caravans. These were some of first caravans we could consider as recreational vehicles. These wealthy Britons used these caravans for short forays into the country-side which they called "Gypsy Outings." This gave them a taste of the carefree life-style.

Fast forward to the 20th century, camp-cars and house cars emerged. Some were designed to simply carry camping gear and supplies. The Ford model T chassis provided a platform for many home-built house cars. The body work and furniture were owner built or custom made by a local coach builder. Many included kitchenettes and even toilet rooms. These were the forerunners of today's motor homes.

During the Great Depression many families took to the road in search of work, living in their cars or trucks. This came to an end with WWII; suddenly everyone had a job or was off to war. The war effort consumed America; camping and other pleasant past times took a back seat. At the end of that Great War families were scrambling to find housing and jobs to support themselves. America was gearing up for a whole new era. There was a population explosion and unprecedented industrial growth.

The RV Life Style

In 1952, a popular singer Diana Shore was starring on a nationally televised variety show, sponsored by Chevrolet. Each week Diana Shore would invite all to "See the USA in your Chevrolet." In the early 1950s most families had little disposable income. Family vacations often consisted of travel to visit grandparents, uncles and aunts. Camping was most associated with the Boy Scouts. The term RV had not yet been coined. There was of course "Airstream ". They are probably the most successful, long running maker of campers. Still, camping was not yet a national passion.

Today you can see the USA and much more in a Chevrolet or Ford powered motor home. These companies and Dodge also make great tow vehicles for camping trailers and 5th wheels. There are six categories of Recreational Vehicles: Pop Ups, camper vans, travel trailers, 5th wheels, class C motor homes, and class A motor homes. Pop Ups are really little more than a tent built on a trailer. The roof pops up and bed extensions pop out. This gives them a great deal more living room but the sides are usually canvas or similar material. They afford better weather protection and usually have standing head-room. Camper vans offer somewhat faster, more convenient set up but generally have less actual living space. Some hardy souls living on very small budgets do actually live for extended periods in one of these. Pop-ups, pick-up trucks with slide-in campers, and van campers are only adequate for short term camping.

With a goal of comfortable accommodations for extended living, we need to look at the more substantial RVs. Generally, the travel trailer will be the least expensive and least luxurious. In all cases I would recommend a minimum of 30 feet. At this length two slides will make for comfortable living. For 5th wheels and motor homes, 32 to 36 feet is even better. At these lengths two slides will serve well, without complicating things. One added advantage to having only two slides is that almost everything in the unit will be accessible when the slides are retracted. You will find this a real advantage if only stopping for a single night.

For those of you unfamiliar with the RV terminology a "slide out" or "slide," is a section of a room that can be retracted into the main room. This reduces over the road width to under the legal limit of 8 feet 6 inches. RV manufacturers sometimes design units with directly opposing or over lapping slides. In many cases access to important areas of the unit is denied while the slides are retracted. When you are looking for a unit, have the salesman bring in all slides so you can evaluate usable space and accessibility under these conditions.

The motor home and 5th wheel makers seem to be indecisive about how big and how many slides are necessary. At this writing, the latest craze seems to be "full wall slides." This must surely require some fancy engineering to maintain structural integrity. When looking at RV floor plans, be sure to note the space actually gained with each slide extended. Most of the "full wall" slides do not extend very far, yielding only a small gain in usable living space. Most of the two slide designs give equal or greater living space than the "full wall" designs. These two slide (one side) designs offer less of a challenge to the engineer and should be more solid down the road. Some have designed two large slides (one each side) with one forward and one aft. This offers a lot of versatility to the designer but does make for a larger unit footprint. Each slide requires its own drive motor and extending / retracting mechanism. Thus, the more slides, the more complicated, the more that can go wrong. It is my belief that some RV makers only want to grab your attention by offering more slides. Recently one proud RV maker announced "the first unit with 6 slides" That's three times the headaches I want. That design must have 3 slides on each side. Who will be the first to design a 7 slide RV? After all, they can put a slide out the back!

Looking at it practically, every slide is a hole in the wall that is difficult to seal against the weather and also adds exterior wall surface. The more slides the harder it will be to heat and air condition. Let's face it, more than four slides may be a challenging LEGO exercise but offers more draw-backs than advantages. Remember each slide adds 800 lbs. to 1,000 lbs. to the weight you will have to carry around. Slides also add to initial cost and could add tremendously impact repair cost.

In choosing between a trailer (either travel or 5th wheel) and a motor home, you should consider the number of times you hope to move locations. If you will spend longer periods (two months or more) in one place, then a trailer may be for you. If however, you want to move on to new places frequently, then a motor home might be for you. In either case, you will no doubt be towing something. Some motor homers manage with bikes or a motor scooter. This will seriously restrict your mobility away from your RV. Travel trailers and 5th wheelers can use their tow vehicle to get around.

If you have chosen a motor home as your travel vehicle, you will need a "dinghy." This can be a small car, small truck, or an SUV towed behind the motor home. I emphasize small, since you will want to maximize the economy of your runabout transportation to offset the cost of operating the motor home. When selecting a "dinghy", sometimes called a "towed" and pronounced TOAD, be sure you can tow it on its own wheels. If not, then you will need a trailer or dolly wheels for towing. One jolly RV owner placed a sign on the back of his dinghy that said "I GO WHERE I'M TOWED".

In the case of travel trailers of 30 feet, you might get by with a ½ or ¾ ton pick-up truck as your tow vehicle. With a larger 32 to 36 foot 5th wheel you will need a ¾ ton or 1 ton truck. At ¾ or one ton, you will have to choose between a gas powered or diesel powered truck. Since this will also be your off site transportation, the added cost of a diesel may be justified. With a diesel engine your fuel mileage will be at least 20% better and diesels have been known to go as much as 500,000 miles, before overhaul. The engines themselves seem almost indestructible. Anything hung on these engines may not have the same longevity. For example: power steering pumps, alternators, even transmissions could fail before the engine. At 160,000 miles we had to replace the turbo charger. At 170,000 miles the rear end gearbox had to be rebuilt. On the plus side, we still get excellent fuel millage and we religiously avoid salty roads and snow. At 250,000 miles the truck still looks great! Those repairs cost a lot. So we looked at replacing the truck only to discover that, this great truck had depreciated some $30,000. A new truck would have an original cost of at least $50,000. This knowledge made our truck look really good. Truck design somehow seems to age more gracefully than car design.

Power Choice

Diesel engines will cost a lot more than gas engines and in many cases you must order a more expensive vehicle just to have the diesel option. On the other hand the heavier units will require a heavy duty diesel. Let's say that you are looking at a weight class that will allow use of either gas power or diesel power. It will cost you at least $20,000 to $50,000 more to option that diesel engine. On the plus side, the diesel will get 20% or better fuel mileage and the engine will run much longer before overhaul those things hung on that diesel will not. The alternator, power brakes, power steering, etc. will be no better than those on a gas engine. They will have about the same life expectancy. Diesel engine maintenance will be more expensive. For instance they will require 2.5X to 3X more oil at every oil change. Their fuel filters will be much more expensive, just to name a few things. Eight to ten years ago diesel seemed the way to go. Now fuel prices are at best equal to or higher than gas prices. The EPA has dictated the addition of "Stuff," attempting to control the emission of pollutants. Because this area is in a state of flux, each person will have to evaluate what will yield the best results for them. Gas powered vehicles on the other hand will cost less at the onset and routine maintenance will be less expensive. Fuel millage will be lower, but you can buy a bunch of gas for the $20,000 to $50,000 difference. If you want the Rolls-Royce of RVs then you will have to pay Rolls Royce prices.

Before you buy a diesel truck, a few cautionary notes are in order: diesel engines do not provide the engine breaking enjoyed by their gas counter parts. So an exhaust break (often called a Jake Brake) is highly recommended. This accessory will pay for itself in reducing brake repair bills and eliminating most of the downhill white knuckle experience. Actually the exhaust brake provides better control than can be achieved with a gas engine. We have the Pack Brake brand and at about 160,000 miles we had to replace the front brake pads for only the second time and have never had any repair to the rear brakes. In my experience that is phenomenal!

When shopping for any RV, keep in mind you will probably get the most for your money by selecting a middle priced unit. The most luxurious tend to be over-priced. A cheap one is usually made cheaply and will show signs of wear and abuse early on. To a point, you get what you pay for. Know the market. On any of the RVs mentioned you should get a minimum of 20% off sticker, and as a first time buyer without a trade-in, you should do much better! Dicker until you don't think they will go any lower. When the salesman really looks like he or she has bled enough, make your offer another $1000 lower. You can always come up.

When researching for an RV purchase, it is very useful to actually tour the manufacturing facility. In fact I would suggest touring more than one, so you can make comparisons. While great floor plans tend to sell RVs, quality construction and quality components are the most important. The industry seems bent on dazzling you with wild graphics, mirrors, and strange upholstery fabrics. Much more important is useful storage and a lot of it. When you approach an RV or enter one and the color, graphics, or fabrics hit you in the face........run for your life. Ugly lasts forever!

Before purchasing a new RV take a serious look at the pre-owned market. Many times you can find a great deal on a slightly used RV. Don't be afraid to travel some distance to look at a prospective purchase. Check the internet for availability of the type you are looking for. Call the owner or dealer in advance with a list of "must have / don't want." Some of the best deals can be found at "destination locations," such as Florida, Texas, Arizona, and California. Occasionally folks get carried away with the idea of living on the road only to find out it's not for them. One way to avoid this might be to rent a motor home for a month before you jump in with both feet.

Since we are trying to maximize our investments and minimize our spending, we must never lose sight of depreciation. All RVs will depreciate as will cars and trucks. Take a very hard look at the initial cost and consider it will depreciate a lot in 10 years. If you still get more than 20% of the purchase price, after ten years of ownership consider it "found money." The condition of the unit will definitively make a difference here.

Medium priced units represent good layouts and a good value. Some have up-scale solid surface counter tops and china toilets and are nicely finished. The middle range motor home will have many of the features of the luxury one and you can add options up to much the same level and still be $20,000 less than the luxury unit.

My choice would be a 32 to 35 foot motor home. There are some very livable floor plans in this range and some can accommodate a washer and dryer. You can have almost anything but a dishwasher or garbage disposal. Even these items can be installed in the mega-buck units. Some appliances are not cost efficient if you want to live in the desert, or other remote area, and save money using solar as your primary source of electric power. With enough solar panels and enough batteries you could probably run a washing machine, but probably not a dryer.

Many people choosing the RV life style consider a washer and dryer to be a luxury. Actually they will save you money and time. Use of a generator for running the washer and or dryer while in the desert, or other remote area, will certainly work if you have water available. Clothes do dry fast in the low humidity of the desert so they can hang outside to dry. Hanging jeans and heavy shirts to dry in your RV will bring up the humidity. Your skin will not feel quite so dry. The moisture also helps avoid sore throats and nose bleeds.

Want to get a big bang for your travel buck? Select an RV that has good storage, space for a washer and dryer and comfortable living accommodations. Plan your trips to allow camping away from the expense of a campground. This is known as "dry camping." Selecting an RV with large fresh water and waste water capacity, will allow you to dry camp for periods up to 10 days. To do this you will have to learn some discipline in your use of both water and electric. Showers will have to be what's called a "Navy Shower." That means wet down, stop water, soap up, then rinse off. You will also have to learn to turn off all electrical lights / appliances that are not actually in use. After about 7 to 10 days of dry camping, spend a day or two in a full hook-up pay-to-play campground. Here you can get that long hot shower, do the laundry and dump your waste tanks. Also check out National Parks and State Parks many of these have "dry camping" with dump and water fill sites. These will allow you to complete many of those chores not feasible out in the "Boon Docks." Most National and State Parks offer Senior Discounts. Remember where ever you go ASK for whatever discount could apply to you, especially those Senior Discounts. Those "kids" at the window rarely think about senior discounts.

Your destination may be several hundred miles away and your time allotted for a particular trip will not allow you to have lengthy stops in route. Why spend your money on campgrounds? Some states allow overnight parking at rest stops and truck stops. Some retailers allow overnight parking, Wal-Mart and Cracker-Barrel to name just two. If you see a large un-populated parking lot it may be your "camp ground" for the evening. You can always ask! A little shy about asking? The only way bashful people live rich are those whose wealthy uncle left them his money. Don't forget the state, county fairgrounds and some city parks. Many allow free self-contained camping, while others charge a small fee. Hayes, Kansas has free camping, while Carey, North Carolina has a fee.

To Live Rich you have to "Think Poor." That is to say, when contemplating anything with a cost, consider how you would achieve that goal if you did not have sufficient cash at hand. Can I do this thing for less? Dicker – Dicker! One of my favorite economic theories is a penny saved is a penny earned. In his time Ben Franklin was right! Let's bring that theory into modern times. "A dollar saved is equal to about $1.50 earned." Now that is not fuzzy economics. Think about it. You earn $1.50 then after Federal, State, local taxes, Social Security, Medicare and credit card fees you are lucky if you can receive one dollar in goods or services!!! When you do it yourself, you don't have to tip someone 20%. So you could say you earned as much as $1.75 by doing it yourself or shopping around for the best price.

If you have a bit of the rolling stone outlook and want to travel a lot, here's how. Plan your travel to include a week to 10 days of dry camping ending with a 2 day stay in a full service campground. While there you can dump your waste water and take on fresh water. This is a good time to get the laundry done. If you don't have a washer or dryer aboard most full service camp grounds have the pay to play kind. There may be a nearby Laundromat. If you have a good mail forwarding service you should call ahead and have your mail sent to the campground, or to general delivery at a near-by Post Office.

There are some organizations you should consider joining. The Good Sam RV club; is like AAA for RVers. They will provide road service, and offer insurance for your RV and/or tow vehicle. Should you have a break down or flat tire out in the middle of nowhere they will send help that is actually equipped to HELP! Many RV manufacturers also sponsor RV clubs for owners of their products. These groups can be a great source of information to help you get the most pleasure and utility from your RV. These groups often have events for members that will include how-to seminars. Some of these seminars are put on by vendors or other highly knowledgeable people.

The RV 1

The floor plan for a motor home depicted here is not one that is currently in production. It is rather a compilation of several I have seen together with ideas for RV living gained over the years. As shown it could be a front engine gas or diesel driven unit. It would be suitable for long term occupancy.

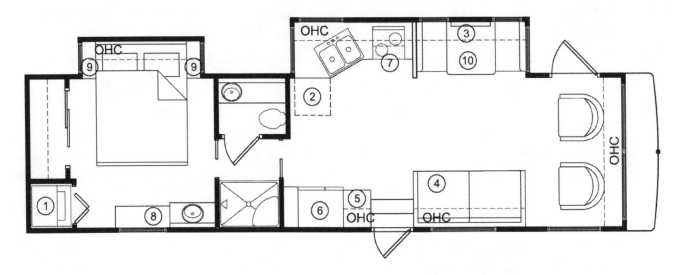

1. STACKED WASHER & DRYER
2. FOLD DOWN COUNTER EXTENSION
3. LED-LCD TELEVISION
4. 74" JACKKNIFE SOFA
5. COUNTER WITH DRAWERS BELOW
6. REFRIGERATOR
7. CONVECTION OVEN ABOVE STOVE
8. HI-BOY CHEST OF DRAWERS
9. NIGHT STANDS
10. DINETTE WITH LEAF AND 2 FOLD UP CHAIRS
OHC = OVER HEAD CABINET

The RV 1

©

Design # 9-003.101
Heated Square Feet: 332
Width: 8'4" Plus Slides
Depth: 34'- 11"
Bedrooms: 1
Bath: 1

Gypsies in the Twenty First Century

Webster's number two definition for Gypsy is: "one inclined to a nomadic way of life." For more than sixty years Americans have been in an almost constant motion chasing employment either of their own volition or moved by a company. Even the federal government seems intent on stirring the pot. Many of those people that have refused to be more mobile have stunted their employment possibilities. During the great depression of the 1930's whole families were packed into jalopies and traveled in search of work. While "gypsy-like", these are not really Gypsies. They only travel in search of more permanent work and will normally settle in the place they find employment.

For the real Gypsies the road is their home. There are the classical Gypsies, whole families traveling together, living and working "on the road." Their homes are often older RVs bursting at the seams with personal possessions and work items. Many tow large utility trailers behind. They are stuffed with products they hawk at county fairs, car shows and other such events. Others have food vendor trailers. Most of these folks probably do not consider themselves as Gypsies, yet they fit the definition.

Lastly there are those known as RV Full-Timers. It is okay folks, you can be proud to call yourself a Gypsy. In the twenty-first century the old stigma of the dishonest Gypsy should not apply to you. Many of you get to spend more time with your far flung families and friends than do those anchored by their brick and stick homes. You can also save on taxes and other repetitive house hold expenses. All the while, seeing parts of this great land you might otherwise miss entirely.

First let's address the two things which worry most want-a-be Gypsies. The easy one is "how do I get my mail?" Having a family member you can trust to sort and forward mail in a timely manner is the easiest way. Yet, while the cheapest it is not necessarily the best. Better way is to have a mail forwarding service handle this chore. It will cost you but ours has more than earned their small fee. Florida, Texas, and South Dakota are three States that are friendly to those that travel full-time.

When we first hit the road one of our first stops was St. Brendan's Isle 413 Walnut St., Green Cove Springs, FL 32043 a great mail forwarding service. A second mail forwarder is: Escapee Mail Service 101 Rainbow Dr. Livingston, TX. 77399. A third out of South Dakota is: Alternative Resources, 3700 South Westport Ave. Sioux Falls, SD 57106

The other worry many people have about living a Gypsy's life style is: what if you or your partner gets sick. Life is full of what-ifs. Don't let them stop you! You should have the same health insurance on the road you would at home. If you are over sixty-five your Medicare will follow you. Be sure any supplement you buy in to is totally mobile. Generally HMO insurance is far less mobile than PPO insurance.

Stuff happens and you can find the strength to deal with it. On one occasion while on the road my wife had difficulty breathing. Long story short, she was hospitalized and had open heart surgery. We found a way to deal with it, even though it delayed our trip about eight weeks. One good thing about living in an RV is you can relocate to be nearer to the hospital if necessary. Just get the patient in good hands first. Even in the 21st century people are really very helpful in these situations. So after eight weeks it was back on the road to Arizona!!

Because we have covered much of the how-to in Living on the Road we will target the minimalist approach. When you get to the down and dirty, what exactly will it take to become a 21st century Gypsy? First and foremost it will require both partners committing to make the idea work. If one has any reservations this is the time to resolve those issues before spending a dime. In this life style you will have to do everything possible... YOURSELF! Knowing this, your plans should be aimed at making chores as simple as possible. For those repetitive chores you should research any devices that will help yet not complicate and be cost effective. For example, most all travel trailers have leveling jacks. Some have as many as four. This can require a lot of hand cranking, detrimental to both elbows and shoulders. The simple economical solution is a cordless drill motor with an appropriate socket fitted; this will do the work for you. The drill motor and a set of drills should be a part of every Gypsy's tool kit in any event. Thus the addition of the socket and adapter will be a very cost effective work saving device. From my experience, I would recommend at least a strong 3/8's drill motor set, with two or more batteries and a charger. This is one of those places not to "cheap-out." I use a half inch drive drill motor, but then I also raise the Sail on my boat with it.

Another handy tool most people would not think of is a wheel ramp. This item can be purchased at Camping World. Got a flat on your Gypsy camper? Changing that tire is lots easier, just drive up on the ramp with the good wheel in front or behind the flat. The bad wheel and tire will rise enough to allow you to make the change. On one occasion we had a flat discovered while exiting a National Park. I called for road service. While waiting for their arrival I decided to try this tool. The tire was changed and we were ready to roll before the service truck had left the garage. Though the service would have been free, we saved an hour or more wait time.

Elsewhere in this book I have been rather emphatic about having a washer / dryer in an RV. Now is the time I will reverse myself. The Gypsy camper here-in described is really too small to accommodate those appliances and too costly. Air conditioning is on the edge of falling into this category. Though most of us have lived with it much of our life, it is not a necessity. You may find that by carefully planning your destinations to locate in cooler climes during the summer, you don't require it. I would however recommend that you plan ahead. Insure your chosen Gypsy camper is fully prepared to accept installation of a commercially appropriate air conditioner. This would include both electrical connections and a hatch opening for the install. If you really want to try going without, don't let one hot night in 365 deter you.

From this point forward we will be discussing the more classical Gypsy style caravan. We should use that term to identify these mobile shelters. I'm sure you have seen Hollywood's idea of the Gypsy as a flamboyant, colorful dresser. The real Gypsies were no doubt much like that. Many Gypsy Caravans were brightly colored and quite ornate. Have you noted the color and graphics of many of the 21st century RVs, especially high end motor homes? While these two art forms are vastly different they both represent a desire to add some artistic beauty to an otherwise bland box. The Gypsy colorful caravan was painted as personal art. The motorhome on the other hand is the art work of a graphics artist in the employ of the motorhome maker.

A monochromatic Gypsy Caravan would look like a commercial trailer, devoid of personality. So we applaud turning them into personal art. This art can run from wild to mild. A design on the mild side, with well-coordinated color and lacking multi-colored swirls and slashes would be refreshing. The original caravans were not much more than boxy wagons with rounded roofs. Their paint jobs made them stand out.

The floor plan shown is larger than the old Gypsy caravans were, but represents a good plan for the 21st century. It leans heavily on our Hunter design but is six feet shorter, less expensive to build and easier to tow behind a half ton pick-up or full-sized SUV. This design would be best with the tow hitch attached to the bath end. This will allow easy access even while attached to the tow vehicle. For so small a unit we have designed-in a fair amount of storage and kitchen facilities. Both the bath and the living room provide more comfort than is usually expected from so small a space. Thanks again to the use of a Murphy bed. The design should prove good for owner construction or economical construction by a custom builder.

This caravan can be built with a rounded roof, a flat roof, or even a peaked roof with gable ends. You must remain under 13 feet. The side walls can be simply painted plywood siding or modern fiberglass laminate commonly used in the RV industry. For a rustic lodge look you could use Western Red Cedar siding. Obviously the plywood is the cheaper. Painting every 3 to 5 years for such a small building should not be a big deal and will keep it looking fresh.

Touring A 21st Century Gypsy Caravan

Starting with the bath, that shower space allows for either a 32 inch or 36 inch fiberglass unit found at most home supply stores. The 32 inch will leave a little more room for the wardrobe. The toilet should be a composter across from a small vanity. One must-have in the bath area is an effective exhaust fan. When it comes to the kitchen there are choices. If you want a double sink as shown, you will have a little less counter space but there is room for the double. Across the way there is room for an eight to twelve cubic foot refrigerator (RV gas and electric.) Alongside is enough space for a full RV stove/oven. A two burner cook top is shown and could have a microwave above. While ovens are nice to have they are not a necessity. I would recommend having a pressure cooker if you opt–out of the oven. This option will prove well worthwhile when spending time off the electrical grid.

Moving on to the living room / bedroom, that little square with the H represents a marine fire place used to heat this unit. It should be quite efficient and add to the ambiance of this rather cozy home. This particular unit is sold by Dickinson Marine and uses out-door air for combustion. It will not deplete the oxygen from the room air. The Murphy bed, chairs, and table are self-explanatory. The two little boxes on either side of the entry door marked ST, would be best built as drawers with storage doors above. That porch is an option. For simplicity I'd have a set of fold up stairs.

Just to keep things simple and conserve on storage space keep kitchen utensils to a minimum. Dual purpose utensils will help. Let the storage space available determine the number and size of dishes you carry. Remember you still must store food. Having a pickup with a cap can augment the interior storage.

This Gypsy Caravan will serve well as a home on wheels and attract new friends. You will find RVers and campers very friendly and want to know more about your Gypsy Caravan.

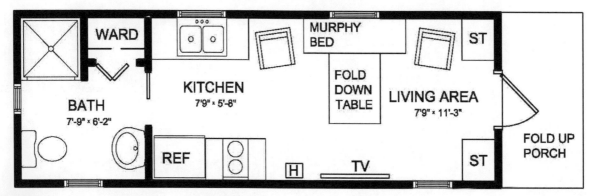

The Gypsy Rose

© CNBdesigns

Design # 9-003.204
Width: 8'4"
Length 24'- 0"

Epilogue

Unless you are the type who reads the last chapter first, you have now been introduced to thinking how to "LIVE RICH ON A SMALL INCOME." We have not attempted to be life coaches, simply open up the concept. As already noted much of your wealth is tied up in your home and cars(s), to which your future income may already be dedicated. These can actually be anchors, keeping you from a fuller life. Keeping the "family home" for the kids is a noble idea, but what about you and your mate? Do you want to sit in an over-sized house waiting for the kids to toss you tidbits of their time? They have their own lives and will be busy-busy…. Kids….Jobs….Friends….Church….Clubs…. and a house of their-own. So how will you have Christmas with them? How about their house or a motel? Don't let your house or your kids turn into that anchor.

What do you really want from life? Travel? Green fees for life? A motorcycle, a boat or unlimited ski lift tickets? Maybe something small like, a "007" Austin Martin? Whatever! You and your mate must look life squarely in the face and make some decisions.

Every time I see one of those commercials that ends with a silhouette of two people in two bathtubs, holding hands. I think to myself "that's really great…but what do they do the rest of the time??" Fulfilling your dream retirement will make those bathtub moments even better.

So let's make a plan A:

#1: Find out just what is our financial state. This will be kind of a state of the union thing.

    A. What would our house bring in the current market?

    B. What is the condition and value of our cars?

    C. Do our kids want our antiques? Do they really want them or will they sell at the most convenient time? What will our antiques bring on the market?

    D. Value all your collections. I know one guy that shared his gun collection with his son who sold them within the year! I know you love your kids, but get real!

    E. Just how will you cover health care cost? There is Medicare and supplements. PPOs travel better than HMO… BUT CHECK! Can you continue your employer's coverage? At what cost? Then of course there is the "Affordable Care Act," but it is untested.

    F. How soon do you want to execute the plan? What impact might this have on the success of the plan?

#2: Where do we go from here? This one may take some time!!

    A. Remember you can have Golf and the Beach at the same time! Some people call it Myrtle Beach!!

    B. Look back at step one and ask yourself: What are we willing to give up in order to have a new beginning?

C. New beginnings do not have to be totally new. They can spring from hobbies, sports, or travels. They become new beginnings when they become the main focus of your life. What trips your trigger?

D. Will a single location actually fulfill your needs and dreams? For many people one location in the right location will be everything they need. Where might that be?

E. While we may represent the extreme, we divide our time between five basic locations. Three are of our choosing and two are mostly to spend time with family. How many do you need?

F. Would a single base of operations and one mobile shelter best fill your needs? How about one of our two bedroom plans and a Gypsy Rose caravan? Or a more economical combination like our Maxi Park and a Gypsy Rose?

G. Are you handy enough to create your own shelter? There are two ways to go here:

    1: Buy a small travel trailer to live in while constructing the major residence.

    2: Have the major residence professionally built and live in it while building a Gypsy.

H. Of course there is always: buy everything, but be careful. Don't pay for what you do not need.

Once having gone through this exercise, make your own list. Freeing up wealth to allow you to redirect it toward other interests is your goal.

Another question needing an answer early on is: Do you want to own real estate or lease? With a two or more bedroom house you will probably have to own the land beneath. With a park model you have the option to lease or own the land. There are at least four, real advantages to the lease option:

1: The lessor will provide the major utilities. These should include electric, water & sewer. Be sure to ask the billing and cost per kilowatt. Some campgrounds make a healthy profit by marking -up commercial rates!

2: When you sign a lease you do not know the landlord, the neighborhood or your immediate neighbors. By lease-end you may want to move and will still have that option. With land ownership not so much.

3: With campground occupancy you can normally move right in. There will be no contacting area government to comply with local zoning laws, or contracting utilities and utility installers.

4: I cannot speak to Mobile Home Park security. It is our experience that campground security is excellent.

5: Be sure to include a smoke alarm with photoelectric technology (P) for "smoldering" first alert as recommended by Fire Departments.

While this is the end of the book, hopefully it will inspire a New Beginning for your life.

References

Barre, Harold. Managing 12 Volts. Incline Village, NV: Summer Breeze.

BNB Designs. Murrells Inlet, SC, 2013. Illistrations,
    Contact Information: Address: P.O. Box 1851 Murrells In let, SC 29576;
    Email: bnbdesigns@sccoast.net; Phone:(843) 424 – 1167

Keidter, Douglas. Mobile Mansions. Layton, UT: Gibbs Smith, <www.gibbs-smith.com>.

Shafer, Jay. The Small House Book. <www.tumbueweedhouse.com>.

Taylor, D.S. Live Rich on a Small Income,
    Contact Information: Email: dahouse62@gmail.com

Williams, Dee. Go House Go. <www.portlandalternativedewellings.com>.

Wood, Donald F. RVs & Campers 1900-2000. Hudson, WI: ICONOGRAFIX.

Disclaimer

About the Author

The author was in manufacturing management for many years, including motorhome manufacturing. In 2005 the author gave up the daily grind, paying real estate taxes, and a mortgage. Since then, David and Abby have been Living Rich on a Small Income. They travel more than 8,000 miles around the USA each year. Their reduced cost for housing and frugal way of life has allowed them to maintain a cruising sail boat and even travel in Europe.

Made in the USA
Lexington, KY
15 July 2013